Inspiring and motivational, *41 Will Come* is a must-read for anyone in a season of waiting on God. Chuck Tate is energetic and encouraging in his call to keep pressing on toward the life to which God has called us.

MARK BATTERSON
New York Times bestselling author of *The Circle Maker*; lead pastor of National Community Church, Washington, DC

Chuck Tate has hit a home run with his book, *41 Will Come*. He does an outstanding job illustrating the importance of standing steadfast in faith while awaiting God's promises. *41 Will Come* is abounding in biblical wisdom as well as personal anecdotes that will teach, counsel, and inspire readers to stay the course in the midst of any trial. This book, I truly believe, will fire up all readers and inspire them to do something great for the Kingdom of God.

MATTHEW BARNETT
Cofounder of the Dream Center

If you find yourself searching for hope in the midst of a Noah-like storm or a children of Israel–like desert, this book is for you. With wit and wisdom Chuck Tate explores the powerful lessons and hope found in the biblically symbolic 41st day (or year) of deliverance. It's the day we often fear may never come, but for those of us who follow Jesus, it always does.

LARRY OSBORNE
Pastor, North Coast Church, Vista, CA

41 Will Come will coach any aspiring person to tackle life's daily challenges and live a Christ-centered life with passion and purpose.

JIM LES
Head coach, UC Davis men's basketball team

No matter what battle you're facing, the good news is that a new day is dawning. Chuck Tate serves up a heaping helping of hope in *41 Will Come*. Your soul needs this refreshing perspective and inspirational reminder that God is on your side, loving you even in the midst of trial. Don't miss the chance to be encouraged and uplifted through Chuck's creative storytelling and unique perspective on the Bible.

CHERIE LOWE
Author of *Slaying the Debt Dragon*

41 Will Come is a practical book that will encourage and inspire your faith. Chuck does a masterful job of casting a biblical vision of hope that resonates with the soul. He weaves biblical truth with practical examples in fun, humorous ways. This book will make you laugh and make you think as it enriches your faith in the goodness of God.

JIM POWELL
Lead pastor, Richwoods Christian Church, Peoria, IL; director of 95network

Rare is the opportunity to hold a real gem—something so intimate and inspirational that you can't wait to share it with others. That's how I feel holding this book. I have watched Chuck foster this dynamic message in his personal life for many years. You will find it powerful, refreshing, and life changing!

BOB BEEMAN
Pastor, Sanctuary International

When a wall is standing between you and your dreams, sometimes you need a friend to help you bust through it. Pastor Chuck Tate is such a friend, and this book is your battering ram.

CHAD R. ALLEN
Blogger, creativity coach, entrepreneur

For all who have ever doubted God, struggled with their purpose, faced discouragement, or wondered whether they would survive overwhelming hardship—that would be *all* of us—this book is for you. Chuck masterfully weaves his own story, the compelling stories of others, and narratives from the Bible in a way that encourages us to hold on. Hope is never realized when we quit; it is experienced only when we remember that 41 is coming. I loved this book!

KURT W. BUBNA
Senior pastor, Eastpoint Church, Spokane Valley, WA; author of *Epic Grace: Chronicles of a Recovering Idiot*

Chuck Tate has written a book for all of us who have been in a season of waiting. In *41 Will Come*, you will be encouraged to believe that God is always on time and that his plan will be worked out in your life. Believe me, after reading this book you will—by God's grace—have a "don't quit" spirit instilled inside you.

BENNY PEREZ
Founding pastor of The Church LV, Henderson, NV

41 WILL COME

HOLDING ON WHEN LIFE GETS TOUGH—AND STANDING STRONG UNTIL A NEW DAY DAWNS

CHUCK E. TATE

TYNDALE®
MOMENTUM

An Imprint of
Tyndale House Publishers, Inc.

Visit Tyndale online at www.tyndale.com.

Visit Tyndale Momentum online at www.tyndalemomentum.com.

Tyndale Momentum and the Tyndale Momentum logo are registered trademarks of Tyndale House Publishers, Inc. Tyndale Momentum is an imprint of Tyndale House Publishers, Inc.

41 Will Come: Holding On When Life Gets Tough—and Standing Strong Until a New Day Dawns

Copyright © 2016 by Chuck E. Tate. All rights reserved.

Cover texture by Gabor Monori/Creative Market. All rights reserved.

Author photograph copyright © 2015 by Seth Lowe. All rights reserved.

Published in association with the literary agency of The Fedd Agency, Inc., PO Box 341973, Austin, TX 78734.

Scripture quotations marked CEV are taken from the Contemporary English Version,® copyright © 1995 by American Bible Society. All rights reserved.

Scripture quotations marked ESV are taken from *The Holy Bible*, English Standard Version® (ESV®), copyright © 2001 by Crossway, a publishing ministry of Good News Publishers. Used by permission. All rights reserved.

Scripture quotations marked MSG are taken from *THE MESSAGE* by Eugene H. Peterson, copyright © 1993, 1994, 1995, 1996, 2000, 2001, 2002. Used by permission of NavPress Publishing Group. All rights reserved.

Scripture quotations marked NASB are taken from the New American Standard Bible,® copyright © 1960, 1962, 1963, 1968, 1971, 1972, 1973, 1975, 1977, 1995 by The Lockman Foundation. Used by permission.

Scripture quotations marked NIV are taken from the Holy Bible, *New International Version,*® NIV.® Copyright © 1973, 1978, 1984, 2011 by Biblica, Inc.® Used by permission. All rights reserved worldwide.

Scripture quotations marked NKJV are taken from the New King James Version,® copyright © 1982 by Thomas Nelson, Inc. Used by permission. All rights reserved.

Scripture quotations marked NLT are taken from the *Holy Bible*, New Living Translation, copyright © 1996, 2004, 2015 by Tyndale House Foundation. Used by permission of Tyndale House Publishers, Inc., Carol Stream, IL 60188. All rights reserved.

Scripture quotations marked TLB are taken from *The Living Bible*, copyright © 1971 by Tyndale House Foundation. Used by permission of Tyndale House Publishers, Inc., Carol Stream, Illinois 60188. All rights reserved.

The stories in this book are about real people and real events, but some names have been changed for the privacy of the individuals involved.

Library of Congress Cataloging-in-Publication Data

Names: Tate, Chuck E., author.
Title: 41 will come : holding on when life gets tough—and standing strong
   until a new day dawns / Chuck E. Tate.
Other titles: Forty-one will come
Description: Carol Stream : Tyndale House Publishers, Inc., IL 2016. |
   Includes bibliographical references.
Identifiers: LCCN 2016005618 | ISBN 9781496410559 (sc)
Subjects: LCSH: Consolation. | Numbers in the Bible.
Classification: LCC BV4905.3 .T36 2016 | DDC 248.8/6—dc23 LC record available at http://lccn.loc.
gov/2016005618

Printed in the United States of America

22   21   20   19   18   17   16
7   6   5   4   3   2

To my family . . .

Annette, from our first date—playing putt-putt golf 28 years ago—to almost 20 years of marriage, raising two amazing children, and a crazy church plant that has turned into more than 18 years of ups and downs and twists and turns, you have held on and stood strong. Your love, sacrifice, and support are still holding up my arms. Thank you for helping to make this dream come true. I love you.

Savannah and Ashton, thank you for your love and sacrifice, and for your encouragement along this 41 Will Come *journey. You embraced the vision as your own. You are my joy. Daddy loves you.*

Dad and Mom, you raised me to love Jesus, you sacrificed to show me Jesus, and you exemplified what it means to put faith in Jesus. These pages are the result of your love and guidance. I love you.

To RockChurch . . .

What can I say? It has been an amazing adventure . . . and it's still going. Thank you for believing in me and this vision. You have heard the phrase "41 will come" more than anyone else . . . and you've embraced it. Your kind words and encouragement pushed me, inspired me, and held me accountable. I love you.

CONTENTS

PATs AND POSTPONED DREAMS

For forty days the rain poured down without stopping.
And the water became deeper and deeper.
GENESIS 7:17-18, CEV

Don't give up and be helpless in times of trouble.
PROVERBS 24:10, CEV

As I PARKED MY CAR outside the Peoria Civic Center and pushed through the humid air toward the arena, I had no idea that God was about to blow my mind. As team chaplain for the hometown Pirates of the fledgling Indoor Football League, I thought I was there simply to give a pregame chapel talk before the Pirates went to war with the Dayton Skyhawks in the semifinals of the league play-offs. At stake was a berth in the first-ever Gold Cup game.

I was locked, loaded, and ready to throw down my 10-minute devotional—an inspiring message about the biblical significance of the number 41, which I had originally intended to use as my season-opening chapel talk. In about two hours, it would become crystal clear why I had put it off each week until this soon-to-be-memorable night.

After the players had gathered, I opened the chapel time with prayer and began to unpack my theme. Perhaps you've heard a sermon or two about the significance of the number 40 in the Bible, but this talk was specifically about the number that comes *after* 40. Here it is in a nutshell:

After Noah built the ark, it rained for 40 days and 40 nights. Day 41 came, and the rain stopped.

After Moses committed murder, he hid in the desert for 40 years. Year 41 came, and God gave Moses a second chance—commissioning him to rescue Israel from slavery in Egypt.

After the Exodus, the children of Israel wandered in the wilderness for 40 years. Year 41 came, and a new generation entered the Promised Land.

For 40 days, Goliath bullied and taunted Israel, just begging for someone to come fight him. Day 41 came, and David stepped up and slew the giant.

For 40 days, Jonah delivered a message of doom and gloom to the city of Nineveh—that God was going to destroy them because of their wickedness. Day 41 came, and God changed his mind and instead extended mercy because the Ninevites had responded and repented.

After being baptized in the Jordan River, Jesus fasted in the desert for 40 days and was tempted by the devil. Day 41 came, the devil fled, angels showed up, and Jesus launched his monumental ministry.

The pattern is clear. The number 41 represents the dawn of a new day—the hope and promise that if you don't quit, the rain will stop, the giant will fall, and you will enter your "promised land."

God believes in second chances.

Your fulfilled vision is right around the corner.

Your 41 will come.

Now fast-forward to the end of the game. Peoria leads by seven points with less than a minute to play. But then Dayton slices through the Pirates' defense and scores another touchdown. All they need is the point after to send the game into overtime.

Extra points in arena football, like extra points in the NFL, are almost automatic. But not this time. To everyone's surprise, and the home team's sheer jubilation, Dayton's kicker did the unthinkable: He missed!

The stadium was instant bedlam. Our guys had just won a smashmouth arena football game, an intense battle that ushered them into the championship game in their very first season!

Final score? Peoria 41, Dayton 40.

That's right: *41 to 40*.

Diving over the box seats behind the press table, where

I had been sitting, I stormed the field—along with almost everyone in the arena—to join the mayhem and congratulate the players.

"Forty-one came tonight, man! Great job, baby!" I screamed at every player I encountered. I was so caught up in winning the game and advancing to the championship that I wasn't even thinking about the score, but only about the breakthrough these guys had achieved after a season of hard work and sacrifice.

In every case, the response was the same—a long pause as the final score collided with the theme of our pregame chapel talk; a half-cocked, crazy grin, as if to say, "Are you kidding me!" and then a boisterous series of "*woot, woot, woot*s!" followed by fist bumps and chest bumps.

Let's be clear: My short chapel talk was not the reason we won that game. But God used it, in that mysterious way of his, to speak to the players, the coaches, and me. By the time we're done here, I hope he will have spoken to you, as well.

Whether you're stuck in the storms of life; in serious need of a second chance; stranded in the wilderness of unexpected circumstances or unfulfilled expectations; facing what seems to be an unbeatable giant; or bearing up against unspeakable temptation, I have two words for you: DON'T QUIT!

As much as you may feel like giving up or giving in, please *don't do it*. Don't go under. Don't throw in the towel. You can hold on and stay strong. Eventually, the rain will stop, an oasis will appear, grace and mercy will be extended, your giant will fall, and a new day will dawn. Forty-one will come.

God can use anyone.

God can use anything.

Even an arena football game.

Even the circumstances in your life.

Trust him. Forty-one will come.

41: A BEACON OF HOPE

Growing up in church, I heard a lot of sermons preached with an emphasis on the number 40. Numerous passages in the Bible connect the number 40 to periods of trial, testing, or hardship. Though there's nothing magical or mystical about the number—some people place too much significance on biblical numerology—it comes up often enough throughout Scripture that we should sit up and take notice. But that's not our purpose here. Instead, we're going to zero in on a number that gets a lot less attention—the number that comes *after* 40. We're going to see how the number 41 represents a beacon of hope for postponed dreams and promised lands. Amid the troubles of everyday life, it's almost as if 41 is shouting, "I got next!"

In the Bible, the number 40 signifies relentless rainfall and neverending storms. (Just ask Noah.) Forty-one resuscitates hope, restores the sunlight, and returns the calm after the storm.

Forty exemplifies exile in the far reaches of a scorching desert, with no end in sight. Forty-one wipes the slate clean and gives birth to second chances.

Forty symbolizes the consequences of bad decisions and disobedience—and the postponement of promised blessings. Forty-one turns the page on a new chapter, a new calling, a new beginning. Forty-one turns what seemed like a pipe dream into a reality.

Forty implies fear and failure, and it represents the devil's best efforts to disrupt, distract, and destroy the work of God. But 40 also represents times of preparation, as God lays the groundwork for the good works he will one day set before us to walk in.

Jesus fasted and prayed for 40 days before launching his earthly work. On day 41, he initiated a ministry unlike any other. Forty-one paved the way for teaching, healing, and miracle after miracle—culminating in the greatest miracle of all. When Jesus rose from the dead, humanity was redeemed, salvation came, and hope was rekindled.

Forty-one turns the page on a new chapter, a new calling, a new beginning.

During the 40 days after his resurrection, Jesus appeared to his disciples on several occasions—proving to them that he was alive and breathing new life into them as he explained the Kingdom of God and commissioned them to build it. On day 41, after promising to send the Holy Spirit in his place, he ascended into heaven, leaving the disciples to carry out his plan for launching the church—a church that, by the way, is still prevailing against the gates of hell.

STAND FIRM AND TAKE ACTION

In the chapters that follow, we're going to take a closer look at one of my favorite "41 Will Come" stories in the Bible— the story of David's epic encounter with the giant named

Goliath. In the process, we'll learn how to knock down the giants that stand between us and the 41 that is out there for us. As the prophet Daniel says about times of trouble, "The people who know their God shall stand firm and take action."[1]

Maybe you've been stuck in a downpour or lost in the desert for what has seemed like 40 years. Maybe you're hiding from an enormous giant—or running away as fast as you can. Maybe you're so hungry for God to move in your life—or in the life of a son, daughter, mother, father, other family member, or friend—that you can taste it, but it feels as if it's never going to happen. Do you feel so spiritually empty that you desperately need a fresh start? Have you just about given up on the future because you feel stuck and defined by your past? Here's the good news: The story's not over. Forty-one is still out there.

"Forty-one will come" is a declaration of faith that things will get better, the rain will stop, the sun will shine, the day will break, the page will turn, the answer will show up, the pipe dream will become reality, the Promised Land will be inhabited, and the giant will fall.

We serve a God who is big enough to restore relationships, heal bodies, extend provision, change circumstances, breathe new life into any situation, and wipe out our sin and the shame associated with it.

And not only is God big enough to save you; he also wants to do it. His desire is to deliver, heal, restore, and redeem you. He wants to set you free.

God's desire to heal is made plain in the story about the

leper who approaches Jesus with a desperate plea for help. This outcast of society walks right up and says, "Lord, if you are willing, you can make me clean."[2]

I love what Jesus does next. He touches the untouchable.

God's desire is to deliver, heal, restore, and redeem you. He wants to set you free.

Think about how huge that is! Jesus touches a leper. He touches an outcast. He touches someone who is considered unclean. But it isn't only the touch that grabs the heart of this particular leper. It's what Jesus says next that changes everything: "I am willing."

Here's the good news: Jesus was willing then, and he's willing now. And not just to make us clean, but also to empower us to overcome the obstacles in our lives and to help us walk by faith the path he has set before us.

Are you ready? It's no accident that you're reading this book. My prayer for you is that you will be challenged, inspired, and encouraged—and more than anything else, that your faith in Christ will make you strong and *keep* you strong so that, when the dust settles after the storm, you will still be standing.

Let's make this personal right from the get-go. Post something on Facebook that you're trusting God for, and use the hashtag #41WillCome. Join the conversation on Twitter by sharing your declaration of faith that things will get better, and use the hashtag #41WillCome. Or post a picture on Instagram, sharing an image of hope for the future—or maybe an inspirational quote or verse—along with the hashtag.

Now, given your current circumstances, what would your "41" look like? Write it here:

_____

#41WillCome

2

FEE FI FO FUM

For forty days, every morning and evening, the Philistine champion strutted in front of the Israelite army.

1 SAMUEL 17:16, NLT

The greater the obstacle, the greater the glory.

MOLIÈRE

ONE OF THE FIRST POEMS I memorized as a kid came from a classic story about facing a giant: "Jack and the Beanstalk."

Fee fi fo fum,
I smell the blood of an Englishman,
Be he alive, or be he dead,
I'll grind his bones to make my bread.

Chances are, you've gone head-to-head with a giant at some point in your life. If so, you know firsthand what defeat feels like. A giant can be anything from a financial crisis to cancer to the big jerk in seventh grade who won't leave you alone. It can be whatever stands between you and your family, you and your dreams, or you and your hope. A giant can even be that voice in your head that whispers, "You can't" or "You won't" or "You never will."

Here's a sad reality: No matter how young or old you are, you haven't seen your last giant. Your enemy, the devil, is doing everything he can to place giants between you and your dreams; between you and your God-given vision; between you and your miracle; between you and your victory; between you and your second chance; and, ultimately, between you and your destiny.

In 1 Samuel 17, we meet a giant bully named Goliath, who has taunted the nation of Israel for 40 consecutive days, just begging for someone to come fight him. The constant jeering has all but paralyzed King Saul and his army.

Have you ever been bullied? Not fun, is it? Maybe you shudder just thinking about it. I love sports, but I remember dreading gym class in seventh grade because I knew I was going to get pounded. Every single day, without fail, this, um, upstanding young citizen would pummel my arm and give me whatever the bicep equivalent of a charley horse is. He wasn't even that big or that tough, but it was as if he had a magical power of intimidation over me.

He always approached me with a smile on his face (that I would have loved to knock down his throat), and his rock-hard knuckles would connect with my arm and ricochet off the bone, sending shock waves of grief pulsating through my entire body.

This happened every stinkin' day.

He thought it was funny. I thought it would be funny if

he never showed up at school again. I dreamed about switching schools or missing the bus, but most of all, I dreamed of punching him in the face. But you know what I did instead?

Nothing.

You know whom I told about it?

Nobody.

Why?

Fear. I was terrified.

Another time, when I was in grade school, my friend Johnny and I were being bullied by some neighborhood punks who stood on the opposite side of the fence that separated the playground at the public school from the grounds of the Christian school that Johnny and I attended. It was like good versus evil. Well, not really, but that's how I felt.

"You guys wanna fight?" my fed-up and overconfident friend shouted to the two bullies.

Uh-oh. Though we were sick and tired of being threatened and called hurtful names, the truth was that I *didn't* want to fight. In the words of Rodney Dangerfield from the movie *Back to School,* "I'm not a fighter. I'm a lover."

Unfortunately, the two punks vaulted over the fence faster than Spider-Man can climb a building. It was crystal clear they intended to accept our challenge.

Once they were on our side of the fence, we backed our way into the fighting arena—aka the church courtyard. As they stared us down, I apprehensively set the rules, even though I had never been in a fight before in my life.

"No weapons!" I barked. They responded by emptying their pockets of knives. True story.

"You take the big one and I'll take the short, scrawny one," I whispered to Johnny. Nothing else was said.

The earth stood still as we gawked at our tormentors. Even though I was probably close to wetting my pants, I decided to make the first move. With a clenched fist, I swung as hard as I could. But just before my fist connected with the other guy's face, I opened my hand and slapped him.

Smack.

Yes, you read that correctly. I know what you're thinking: *Dude! You just surrendered your man card.*

I believe he was more stunned than I was because he looked at me as if to say, *Seriously, bro?*

You're probably laughing at me right now. I'm laughing at myself. Then I completely baffled him by apologizing.

"I'm sorry, man. I don't want to fight."

I would love to tell you that he was so impressed with my change of heart that he said, "It's all good. Let's be friends and ride bikes."

Nope.

Even though I said that I was sorry and I didn't want to fight, it was too late—and it was about to get ugly.

While I was slapping my tormentor, my friend Johnny—unbeknownst to me—had taken off running, leaving me alone with the two thugs. After I had finished apologizing, the big one grabbed my arms from behind so his friend could unleash an unbridled blow to my face.

Game over.

I ran home crying. A black eye followed. And from that day on, I was afraid to ride my bike alone.

Perhaps this is why the very first message I ever preached was about David and Goliath. During my fifth-grade year, the same year I got punched in the eye, I represented the Christian school I attended—the same one where I got beaten up—in a regional preaching competition. And I've been preaching it ever since. First Samuel 17 is one of my favorite chapters in the Bible because it offers hope to the underdog. It's a reminder that God will help us fight battles that we could never win on our own.

> God will help us fight battles that we could never win on our own.

You might be in just such a battle right now. Keep reading.

ENTER DAVID. ENTER HOPE.

It was pretty easy for Goliath to mess with the Israelite soldiers because, when you're the biggest and baddest, you don't really expect anyone to fight you. Goliath had conducted his scare-tactics routine for 40 days without a single challenger stepping forward.

I love that the most unlikely contender was the very one to step onto the battlefield and finally accept the giant's challenge. David wasn't only the least likely person in Israel to fight Goliath; he was also the least likely person *in his own family*—the youngest of eight boys.

When you're the youngest of eight, it's easy to get lost in the shuffle. It's easy to be forgotten. It's easy to be left alone. While his brothers had more prestigious duties, such as serving King Saul in the Israelite army, David was left at home to shepherd the sheep. He happened to hear Goliath's defiant words only because he was checking in on his brothers for his dad.

Before David's heroic victory over Goliath, God had sent the prophet Samuel to David's home to anoint one of Jesse's sons as the next king. Samuel did the logical thing, the same thing most people in his position would have done. He made his judgment based on appearance and assumed the chosen one would be the strong and handsome Eliab, Jesse's first-born and David's eldest brother.

God's response was, "No. He's not the one."

Samuel then approached the second eldest. God's reaction was the same: "Nope."

Samuel continued down the line through all seven of David's brothers, and God rejected all of them.

By this point, Samuel had to have been confused, possibly embarrassed, and most likely frustrated.

"Uh, are these the only sons you have?" he asked.

"No," Jesse replied. "I forgot my youngest son, David, but he's out tending the sheep."

For anyone who has ever been overlooked, for anyone who has ever been forgotten (I'm talking *Home Alone* forgotten), for anyone who has ever been lost in the crowd—what happens next delivers a message about confident expectation.

Jesse sent for David. When he came in from the field, the Lord said to Samuel, "This is the one; anoint him."[1]

As David stood among his brothers, who by now were no doubt wondering what was up, Samuel took the flask of oil and anointed him with it. "And the Spirit of the LORD came powerfully upon David from that day on."[2]

So David was anointed as the next king of Israel and went straight to the palace, right? Wrong. He went right back to the sheep. And David's older brothers went off to fight the Philistines.

So you can imagine David's excitement when his father asked him one day to take some food to his brothers on the front lines. Taking a break from the daily grind of shepherding, he went to visit his brothers and get the scoop on the war.

While visiting the battlefront, David got an up-close look at the huge giant named Goliath. He heard firsthand Goliath's defiant challenge to Israel. And David wasn't intimidated. Evidently, he was listening to the Holy Spirit because he embarked on a course of action that no one else would try.

It's important to point out that David heard the very same words that every soldier in Saul's army had heard. The difference was that David decided to do something about it.

When it comes to bullying, have you ever thought to yourself, *Why doesn't somebody do something?* Let me remind you: *You* are somebody. What are you going to do about the bully who stands between you and your victory? What are you going to do about the giant standing between you and your dream? What are you going to do about the obstacle that is keeping you from becoming the person who God created you to be? Are you

> **David heard the very same words that every soldier in Saul's army had heard. But David decided to do something about it.**

prepared to cut through the resistance? Are you ready to fight? I'm not talking about fake fighting. I'm not talking about slapping your enemy. I'm talking about trusting God and stepping onto the battlefield—even when no one else believes you can win—and fighting, if need be, until you are the last one standing. David was that somebody with Goliath. You can be that somebody too.

FIGHTING FOR MY FAMILY

"I'm sorry, honey," the immigration lawyer said matter-of-factly. "Your husband is going to be deported, and there's nothing you can do about it."

I will never forget that somber moment as I sat with my dejected sister, Cherie, and her husband, Eddy. They were still newlyweds, and Cherie was pregnant.

Eddy had been an answer to prayer for Cherie—the man of her dreams, the man she had patiently waited years for. Our family was ecstatic when they got engaged, and I was honored to perform their wedding. Cherie got pregnant on their honeymoon, and just like that, their marriage was off to a fairy-tale start.

A few months later, a letter from Homeland Security brought the honeymoon phase to a screeching halt. The thought of losing her new husband to deportation sent Cherie into a tailspin.

As I looked into my sister's tear-filled eyes, I saw fear. I saw desperation. I saw panic. I felt it myself. And then I got mad. Have you ever felt everything within you rise up like a striking cobra? I wasn't so much angry at the attorney's words as I was upset with her lack of tact and compassion. It wasn't a pleasant meeting, to say the least.

As we got back into the car for our drive home, I looked at Cherie and Eddy and said, "We're going to find a new attorney, we're going to fight this, and we're going to win!" It was as if I had cued up Survivor's "Eye of the Tiger." Little did I know that it would take a whole lot more than an inspirational song; our fight would become an emotional roller coaster—consisting mostly of downturns—that would last more than six years. Before it was over, the fight would become an all-out war, with many uphill battles that produced only hurt, heartache, and overwhelming anxiety.

Eddy's battle began in Indonesia, where he grew up as part of an ethnic Chinese minority. He experienced discrimination firsthand when he was attacked on a bus by a group of radical extremists. Bloodied and battered, he was dumped in a field and left for dead. This hate-fueled assault prompted Eddy to seek asylum in America, where he went to live with his uncle.

Eddy arrived in the United States with renewed hope and endless possibilities ahead of him. It was a new chapter, a new beginning, a new life.

Everything in America exceeded his expectations—until he inadvertently hired a fraudulent law firm that failed to attend a crucial asylum hearing on his behalf. As a result, Eddy's case was closed, and the life's savings he had spent on legal fees was gone.

After Eddy and Cherie were married, they were granted a marriage petition, and Eddy received a renewed work permit. They hired a new attorney and assumed that their marriage petition would pave the way for Eddy's asylum case to be reopened. Unfortunately, they were denied. They appealed and were denied again.

What happened next delivered a disheartening and devastating blow that all but crushed them. Eddy received a letter with detailed instructions to report to Homeland Security on September 12, 2007, in order to be deported. The letter included size and weight specifications for the luggage he was to bring and a list of belongings he would need for his flight to Indonesia.

You might be thinking, *So he gets deported. It's not the end of the world. His wife can move to Indonesia with him until everything gets cleared up.* If only it had been that simple. By this time, Cherie was seven months pregnant with their first daughter, and the location and living conditions in Indonesia were not suitable for giving birth or raising a baby—at least not by American standards. Eddy had come to America seeking asylum because his life was in danger, and his prospects for finding adequate employment in Indonesia to support his family were not promising.

Before Eddy reported for his deportation, our family—including our church family—prayed for him and claimed the promises of Scripture for him. As I reminded Eddy more than once, "The giant you are facing is going to fall. Forty-one will come!" My sister clung to the following passage in Isaiah and began quoting it and praying it every day:

But now, O Jacob, listen to the LORD who created you.
O Israel, the one who formed you says,

"Do not be afraid, for I have ransomed you.
  I have called you by name; you are mine.
When you go through deep waters,
  I will be with you.
When you go through rivers of difficulty,
  you will not drown.
When you walk through the fire of oppression,
  you will not be burned up;
  the flames will not consume you.
For I am the LORD, your God,
  the Holy One of Israel, your Savior.
I gave Egypt as a ransom for your freedom;
  I gave Ethiopia and Seba in your place."[3]

Eddy packed his bags and flew to Atlanta with my dad and sister, desperate for a miracle. Even now, as I sit in a local coffeehouse recalling that terrifying day, I am moved to tears.

Eddy and Cherie walked into the Homeland Security office, and the agent in charge said, "I have the authority to take you into custody right now and send you back to Indonesia . . ."

Gulp.

"But I'm not going to do that. I'm going to give you another chance to get your case reopened."

They returned home to Illinois, relieved and rejoicing, but the battle was only heating up. In the eyes of Homeland Security, Eddy was not a husband, father, uncle, son-in-law, brother-in-law, church member, friend, employee, and tax-payer. He was a case number, whose story didn't matter.

But God had a different idea. In the words of Perry Noble, pastor of NewSpring Church in South Carolina, "Every number has a name, every name has a story, and every story matters to God."[4] Eddy's story mattered to God, and we believed that God was going to use Eddy's story to encourage other people.

My sister and brother-in-law spent their savings again by hiring a third attorney and filed another appeal to have Eddy's case reopened. Again they were denied—and this time they were informed that it's virtually impossible to have a case reopened.

But we didn't quit.

As time passed, Cherie and Eddy and their two little girls tried to live a normal life in the midst of uncertainty. Flights and road trips to Atlanta and Chicago to meet with lawyers and Homeland Security became frequent. Each meeting ended with disappointment and the sinking reality of Eddy's plight. Eddy's motion to have his case reopened had now been denied four times. There would be no more chances. Finally, Eddy was notified to report to Homeland Security again, where his deportation order would be carried out. He needed a miracle.

The new law firm that represented Eddy advised that his only hope for a reprieve was to create awareness and to appeal to our congressman to intervene on Eddy's behalf. But time was short. We unleashed a campaign we called "The Fight to Save Eddy from Deportation," sharing Eddy's story on Facebook, Twitter, and Tumblr. We produced a YouTube video featuring my niece Jadealynn pleading her father's case. We prayed. My sister contacted our congressmen. We prayed. A petition from Change.org and hundreds of letters to President Obama from our church and our friends followed. We prayed. Interviews with local radio stations and newspapers opened up. We prayed. Our strategic plan to create awareness was in full force as God raised up an army in Eddy's defense.

Not long after the denial of Eddy's fourth and final appeal, as enforcement of the deportation order became imminent, Cherie received another phone call from their attorney in Atlanta—a call that lifted the weight of the world from her shoulders and delivered tears of joy. Somehow, Eddy's story had reached the desk of the Secretary of Homeland Security, and the chief counsel for US Citizenship and Immigration Services had filed a motion to reopen Eddy's case.

Boom!

Instead of reporting to his deportation officer in Chicago with a suitcase packed for Indonesia, Eddy arrived with paperwork to officially terminate the deportation order. He received his green card in 2013 and will be eligible to apply for US citizenship in 2016.

GOD DOESN'T PLAY FAVORITES

I have a plaque on my office desk that reads: *Jesus loves you, but I'm his favorite.* No, I didn't buy it for myself. It was a gift. But I am surprised that I'm the only one in the world who has it.

Okay, I'm kidding.

One of the many things I love about God is that he is no respecter of persons. As the apostle Peter noted after being summoned to the home of Cornelius, a Roman officer, "I see very clearly that God shows no favoritism."[5] What God did for my brother-in-law, Eddy, he can do for you. So go ahead and identify your giant, and get ready to step onto the battlefield.

#41WillCome
#SlayingGiants

3

TOUGHER THAN HELL

The Spirit of the LORD came powerfully upon David from that day on.

1 SAMUEL 16:13, NLT

Life is tough, but you are tougher.

ANONYMOUS

MOST KIDS ARE OBSESSED with superheroes. Heck, a lot of adults are obsessed with superheroes. Batman. Superman. Spider-Man. Iron Man. Captain America. Hulk. Indiana Jones.

Wait a minute . . . Indiana Jones?

Yep.

About twenty years ago, while visiting Florida, my roommate Dave and I stood in a long line at Walt Disney World's Indiana Jones Epic Stunt Spectacular with our boss's three-year-old son, Sumner, who idolized Indiana Jones. We couldn't help but smile at the thought of how Sumner would react when he saw his beloved hero.

After struggling to keep our young charge calm while

waiting in a truly epic line, when the long-awaited moment finally arrived we rushed in, snagged our seats, and prepared ourselves to be wowed. Sumner was on cloud nine, drinking in the spectacular scenery as he waited for the show to begin.

Then something special happened. The actor portraying Indiana Jones asked for a volunteer from the packed-out auditorium, and to our pleasant surprise my roommate Dave was chosen. He reacted as if his name had been called during the first round of the NFL draft. As Dave strutted up to the front, Sumner was close to losing his mind. With the world's widest grin, he looked at me and screamed while pointing at Dave, "Chuck! Look! Dave gets to meet Indiana Jones!" I don't remember much after that, but I know that Sumner had the best time of his three-year-old life.

We went straight from the Epic Stunt Spectacular to the popular Tower of Terror, but Sumner was too little to ride, so I volunteered to hang with him while Dave rode the Tower by himself.

Sumner and I found a concrete bench nearby and talked about what we had just experienced at the Indiana Jones show. Actually, Sumner talked and I listened. Quickly escalating into full-on chatterbox mode, he talked my ear off, punctuating his epic monologue by rapidly swinging his short legs back and forth. The more excited he got, the faster he talked; and the faster he talked, the faster his little legs went. Before I realized what was happening, he was rocking back and forth so fast that he launched himself from the bench like a cannonball and landed with both exposed knees on the concrete.

Ouch!

Convinced that Sumner was about to start screaming bloody murder, I scooped him up, looked into his tear-filled eyes, and said reassuringly, "Man, Sumner! You are as tough as Indiana Jones!" With teeth clenched, he pushed back the tears, swallowed his cry in one giant gulp, stared deep into my eyes, and said with confidence, "*Tougher.*"

TOUGHNESS COMES FROM WITHIN

When David stepped onto the battlefield to confront Goliath, he wasn't measuring himself by his size or his strength. Goliath had him on both counts. He wasn't depending on his qualifications as a soldier or his military experience. He had none. But what he had was an inner toughness and confidence that came from relying on the power of God to deliver him.

How did that happen? Well, God in his wisdom had seen fit to send a lion and a bear to fight David in a couple of undercard matches out in the field when he was tending his sheep. By the time he showed up for the title bout, he wasn't looking at Goliath as a big, bad giant. No, David saw him as nothing more than an "uncircumcised Philistine . . . [who] has defied the armies of the living God."[1] The reason David was tougher than Goliath had nothing to do with his natural abilities and everything to do with the God he served. "There are some things that people cannot do, but God can do anything."[2]

> **What David had was an inner toughness and confidence that came from relying on the power of God to deliver him.**

We need to remember who we are. Let me remind you and encourage you: If the Holy Spirit is inside you, you are tougher than whatever bully is staring you down. "You belong to God, and you have defeated these enemies. God's Spirit is in you and is more powerful than the [spirit] that is in the world."[3]

How has God already prepared you to stand strong in your current season of testing? David's preparation happened when he was a teenage shepherd alone in a field. (And not a teenage mutant ninja shepherd either.) His preparation began while he was the least among his family, doing what seemed to be the most insignificant chore. What a great reminder not to sell yourself short! God sees you differently than others see you. God sees you differently than you see yourself. He wants to use you more than even you desire to be used. His plans for you are greater than you could ever imagine, and they are brimming with hope.[4]

It's easy sometimes to feel overlooked. Do you feel forgotten? Have you been swallowed up by the crowd? It's not very fun to be chosen last, even if it's something as insignificant as gym-class dodgeball. I've never met anyone who enjoys being the last pick. And believe me, I know what it feels like. In one of my high school yearbooks, there is a photo of me sitting on the bench during a soccer game, and the caption reads, "Boy, I wish I was out there."

Ouch.

But David was handpicked by God. *You* are handpicked by God too—and he has some good things planned for you. "We are God's masterpiece. He has created us anew in Christ

Jesus, so we can do the good things he planned for us long ago."[5]

God saw you before you were even conceived. You're not an accident. God has plans, good plans, that he dreamed up for you a long time ago.

The moment that David was anointed as future king of Israel, God's Spirit entered him and empowered him for the future. The Bible also confirms that, if you belong to God, his Spirit lives inside you—which means that you, too, are empowered for your future. Those aren't my words; they're God's words.

> You are controlled by the Spirit if you have the Spirit of God living in you. (And remember that those who do not have the Spirit of Christ living in them do not belong to him at all.) And Christ lives within you . . . because you have been made right with God. The Spirit of God, who raised Jesus from the dead, lives in you. And just as God raised Christ Jesus from the dead, he will give life to your mortal bodies by this same Spirit living within you.[6]

If that doesn't boost your confidence, your booster is broken.

And it gets better. You're not just a conqueror. You're *more than* a conqueror. You're not just tough. You're *tougher.*

> So, what do you think? With God on our side like this, how can we lose? If God didn't hesitate to put everything on the line for us, embracing

our condition and exposing himself to the worst
by sending his own Son, is there anything else he
wouldn't gladly and freely do for us? And who would
dare tangle with God by messing with one of God's
chosen? Who would dare even to point a finger? The
One who died for us—who was raised to life for
us!—is in the presence of God at this very moment
sticking up for us. Do you think anyone is going
to be able to drive a wedge between us and Christ's
love for us? There is no way! Not trouble, not hard
times, not hatred, not hunger, not homelessness,
not bullying threats, not backstabbing, not even the
worst sins listed in Scripture:

> They kill us in cold blood because they hate you.
> We're sitting ducks; they pick us off one by one.

None of this fazes us because Jesus loves us. I'm
absolutely convinced that nothing—nothing
living or dead, angelic or demonic, today or
tomorrow, high or low, thinkable or unthinkable—
absolutely *nothing* can get between us and God's
love because of the way that Jesus our Master has
embraced us.[7]

Now that we know that God has our back, let's identify
our 41. For my brother-in-law, Eddy, 41 represented a judge
reopening his asylum case. For the church my wife and I
planted more than 17 years ago, one of our 41s was acquiring

our own building. My mother's 41 was a healing miracle that I will share about later in the book.

What about you? Perhaps one of the following is your personal 41:

- Freedom from pornography
- Deliverance from alcohol or drug addiction
- Marital restoration
- Reconciliation with a child, parent, other relative, or friend
- Financial breakthrough
- Physical or emotional healing
- Beating cancer
- Waiting patiently on a transplant list
- Job security
- An open door in ministry
- Favor in an upcoming trial
- Receiving a second chance
- Embracing your self-worth
- Winning an election
- Finding faith to dream again
- Overcoming depression
- Finding your life mate
- Making the team
- Getting accepted into school
- Passing an important test

Be encouraged. You are not merely as tough as the giant that stands between you and your 41. You are *tougher*. You are not only a conqueror; you're more than a conqueror. You're a winner. You're the head and not the tail. You're above and not beneath. You're going over and not under! Here's proof:

1. You Are Connected to Christ

This is a simple yet powerful truth. You are connected to Christ. You are connected to the Living Word. You're connected to the Creator of the universe. You're connected to the very one who has already defeated your Goliath. The devil is identified in Scripture as the "prince of this world,"[8] but "you belong to God . . . [and] you have already won a victory . . . because the Spirit who lives in you is greater than the spirit who lives in the world."[9] (#Boom)

2. You Are Empowered by Christ

Not only did Jesus promise to be with us, but he also gave us the authority to represent him on earth. He even empowered his disciples to cast out demonic spirits. That same power belongs to us.

The greatest miracle in history took place when Jesus defeated death and raised himself from the dead. Romans 8:11 reminds us that the same Spirit lives inside you and me. This means that we have resurrection power!

3. The Devil Knows He Can't Stop You

The devil knows that he's already defeated. He knows where he's going, and he knows that you're tougher than he is. The devil is a deceiver. He's good at throwing his weight around, and he uses intimidation to defeat many people.

James 4:7 says, "Resist the devil, and he will flee from you." The first part of this verse says, "Humble yourselves before God."[10] That's the key. Surrender to Jesus, and he will give you hope. Surrender to Jesus, and he will give you the victory.

Jesus said to Peter, "Upon this rock I will build my church, and all the powers of hell will not conquer it."[11]

Jesus died so the church could exist.

Jesus said he's the head of the church.

Jesus said he's the one building it.

Jesus chose the church as the vehicle to advance his Kingdom.

Jesus said that all the powers of hell will not conquer it.

We are the church . . . which means we are *tougher* than hell.

_____

#41WillCome
#TougherThanHell

4

CAN YOU HEAR ME NOW?

While they were talking together, the Philistine champion,
Goliath of Gath, stepped out from the front lines of the
Philistines, and gave his usual challenge. David heard him.

1 SAMUEL 17:23, MSG

The pessimist sees difficulty in every opportunity. The
optimist sees opportunity in every difficulty.

ANONYMOUS

SEVERAL YEARS AGO, a widely viewed television ad for Verizon Wireless popularized the slogan "Can you hear me now?" Verizon understood that nothing is more frustrating than a wireless plan with bad reception and dropped calls: *Hello? Hello? Can you hear me? What? How about now? What about now? Hello? I think I lost you. Ugh.*

The more towers Verizon erected, the fewer dropped calls they had. The fewer the dropped calls, the greater the customer satisfaction. It's all about being able to hear the person on the other end, right? We can't respond if we can't hear.

Sometimes we don't respond because we don't *like* what we hear. That was certainly true of the army of Israel:

[David] arrived at the camp just as the Israelite army was leaving for the battlefield with shouts and battle cries. Soon the Israelite and Philistine forces stood facing each other, army against army. David left his things with the keeper of supplies and hurried out to the ranks to greet his brothers. As he was talking with them, Goliath, the Philistine champion from Gath, came out from the Philistine ranks. Then David heard him shout his usual taunt to the army of Israel.

As soon as the Israelite army saw him, they began to run away in fright. "Have you seen the giant?" the men asked. "He comes out each day to defy Israel."[1]

The Israelite army didn't like what they saw. They didn't like what they heard. Unfortunately for them, they were forced to watch and hear Goliath's taunt for 40 consecutive days—and not just once. "For forty days, *every morning and evening*, the Philistine champion strutted in front of the Israelite army."[2]

Imagine what that must have been like:

- **Day 1:** The giant's epic confrontation catches Israel off guard. They respond with silence.
- **Day 2:** Goliath spews his intimidating and hateful demands. Israel's response is the same: nothing.
- **Day 3:** Same challenge. Same response.
- **Day 17:** By now, perhaps they've learned to look the other way while pretending not to hear.
- **Day 29:** Yada yada. Nada.
- **Day 40:** Silence is the new normal. Silence is the

daily routine. Silence is habit. Silence is the only safe
response—the only *sane* response, or so it seems.

Goliath's persistent posturing and cantankerous words
were a formidable death threat for anyone who ventured out
to challenge him. To add insult to injury, his jeering was
insulting to the God whom Israel served.

Goliath's strategy worked. Israel bought the lie hook, line,
and sinker. They honestly believed there was nothing they
could do. Their silence reinforced their belief that Goliath's
taunting was more than talk.

They *wanted* to take action. I'll bet they voiced their concerns to one another every day as they agonized over their
predicament. In fact, they all were well aware of the reward
for anyone brave enough to fight the Philistine giant and
skilled enough to take him out: "The king has offered a huge
reward to anyone who kills him. He will give that man one
of his daughters for a wife, and the man's entire family will
be exempted from paying taxes!"[3]

But we all know that talk is cheap, and vision without
action is just a pipe dream.

I can picture Goliath cupping his ear (as I do when I'm
struggling to hear someone) and mimicking the Verizon
commercials a few thousand years ahead of his time: "Can
you hear me now? What about now? Any takers?"

Crickets.

By the 40th day, the stalemate itself had gone stale, and
there was no indication that anything would change.

Day 41: Enter one scrappy teenager.

HEAR. LISTEN. RESPOND.

On day 41, Goliath stepped out from the front line of the Philistines—as always—and issued the usual challenge.

David heard him.

There is a difference between not hearing and choosing to ignore. There is also a difference between merely hearing on the one hand and listening and responding on the other.

As my wife, Annette, will tell you, I'm a bad listener. She sees red whenever I attempt to finish her sentences because I assume I already know what she's talking about. I cut her off all the time, only to discover I had no clue what she was going to say. I guess you can say I'm a work in progress.

There is a difference between merely hearing on the one hand and listening and responding on the other.

I'm a bad listener for two reasons. First, I'm usually the one doing all the talking. As a pastor, I preach and teach three times every weekend; I lead several meetings each week and do my share of pastoral counseling and assorted ministerial appointments in between. On top of that, I struggle to listen because I'm hearing impaired. I don't like to think of it as a disability, but I wear hearing aids in both ears. I have to constantly remind myself to let other people know that I wear hearing aids, so they won't think I'm a jerk or an idiot when I ignore them or stare at them with a deer-in-the-headlights look. On the other hand, if you have to repeat yourself more than twice and I still don't hear you, I will agree with almost anything you say. (And yes, this has led to some pretty awkward moments.)

Just the other day, I was returning an item to the hardware store, and for the life of me I could not hear what the clerk was saying. By the third repetition, she was clearly becoming annoyed.

"Are you *daft?*" she said.

Finally, someone who understands me!

"Yes, I wear two hearing aids."

Okay, I'm kidding. She didn't really say that, and I didn't mishear her. She even apologized for her irritation when she found out I couldn't hear. But many times I've been treated as if I'm stupid just because I'm hard of hearing.

However, if I *hear* you, but choose not to *listen* . . . well, that's a different matter.

The soldiers in the army of Israel *heard* Goliath.

The soldiers in the army of Israel *listened* to Goliath.

The soldiers in the army of Israel *responded* to Goliath . . . with *fearful silence.*

David *heard* Goliath.

David *listened* to Goliath.

David *responded* to Goliath . . . with *faithful action.*

Israel ran *away* from the enemy.

David ran *toward* the enemy.

How will you respond to the giants in your life? I want to respond like David. David heard the intimidating words of the enemy, and they motivated him to take action. The army of Israel heard the same words and succumbed to fear.

In the remaining chapters, we'll uncover seven keys in David's story that will help us to move from fear to faith and from indecision to action.

When life gets tough, the first key to holding on and standing strong is to *know your enemy*.

| **Keys to help you hold on when life gets tough and stand strong until a new day dawns** | *1. Know your enemy.* |

KNOW YOUR ENEMY

David knew that Goliath was Israel's enemy. He was aware that Goliath was using scare tactics to cripple the nation of Israel. *David's* nation. God's people. That made Goliath his enemy—an enemy who had to be stopped. But when we face our own giants, it isn't always so obvious who the enemy is.

For example, your enemy is not that coworker who chomps her gum and drives you crazy. Your enemy is not the cranky clerk with the bad breath behind the cash register. Your enemy is not the old man down the road who yells at the neighborhood kids for turning their bikes around in his driveway. Your enemy is not your former spouse, your boss, or that maniac who just cut you off on the expressway on the way to work. (Okay, it might be him.) When we get into a scrape, we tend to focus on the person with whom we're in conflict, but it goes deeper than that. The Bible is pretty clear about this: "We are not fighting against

flesh-and-blood enemies, but against evil rulers and authorities of the unseen world, against mighty powers in this
dark world, and against evil spirits in the heavenly places."[4]
Or as the apostle Peter puts it: "Stay alert! Watch out for
your great enemy, the devil. He prowls around like a roaring
lion, looking for someone to devour."[5]

A lot of people picture the devil as an imaginary character in a red suit, rocking horns and a pitchfork while
laughing it up in hell. But the devil is not in hell. Scripture
confirms that someday he will be cast into a lake of fire,
but until then his strategy is to patrol the earth to steal,
kill, and destroy those who will let him. And sometimes we
are affected by others who are allowing the devil to break
in on them.

This isn't the place for a theological discourse on the exis-
tence of Satan, but suffice it to say that there is a very real
devil, an evil being who prowls the earth looking to steal
from you and kill your dreams, and he would like nothing
better than to utterly destroy you.

Jesus once warned Peter about the importance of vigilance
in the face of the devil's schemes: "Simon, stay on your toes.
Satan has tried his best to separate all of you from me, like
chaff from wheat."[6]

In his first epistle, Peter echoes this warning to the church:

Keep a cool head. Stay alert. The Devil is poised
to pounce, and would like nothing better than to
catch you napping. Keep your guard up. You're not
the only ones plunged into these hard times. It's the

same with Christians all over the world. So keep a firm grip on the faith.[7]

Not only do we need to rely on God and use the armor he provides, but we also need to encourage other Christians: "Keep your eyes open. Keep each other's spirits up so that no one falls behind or drops out."[8]

As a master of deception, the devil will try to get you focused on all the wrong things. At times I have been my own worst enemy because I allowed the devil to whisper in my ear and get into my head. No more!

I love how David got fed up with all the cowardice on display and told his brothers, "I'm here to right this wrong! How dare this uncircumcised Philistine defy our God!"

I want to be like David. How dare we allow the devil to steal from us and from our families? How dare we let him rip us off and keep us from moving forward?

Maybe your giant is anchored in your history. Too many people feel as if they can never get past their past. I want to remind you that the blood of Jesus is sufficient to wipe out your past: "There is no condemnation for those who belong to Christ Jesus. And because you belong to him, the power of the life-giving Spirit has freed you from the power of sin that leads to death."[9]

Are you fed up? Tired of feeling condemned when in fact you've been set free? Identify and slay your giant! It doesn't matter how big it is. God is bigger.

THE ULTIMATE COMEBACK

Not only do we need to be aware of who our true enemy is, but we must also be aware of his schemes. The apostle Paul tells us to put on the full armor of God so we can "stand firm against all *strategies* of the devil."[10] We need to be aware of the devil's strategies so we will know how to combat them. Paul's encouragement to "be strong in the Lord and in his mighty power"[11] is echoed by Peter: "Stay alert! Watch out for your great enemy, the devil. . . . Stand firm against him, and be strong in your faith."[12]

I love that, out of all of Jesus' disciples, it is Peter who warns us about the devil's schemes. If anyone is qualified to give instruction about the strategies of the devil, it's Peter. This is the same disciple who continually inserted his foot into his mouth and who was even called *Satan* by Jesus.[13]

Think about that for a moment. No matter how bad of a day you may be having, at least Jesus hasn't called you Satan, right? Peter is also the same disciple who adamantly told Jesus that he would never deny or disown him, and then did just that—not once, not twice, but three times in the same night. He's like me. He's like you. He's like all of us. Have you ever promised God that you wouldn't do something and then turned around and did that very thing?

Oops! My bad.

The last time Peter saw Jesus before the Crucifixion was right after Peter had cussed out a little girl and denied even knowing Jesus. Then the Lord looked at him, a rooster crowed, and Peter remembered what Jesus had said just a few hours earlier.

Think about the guilt and shame that must have permeated Peter's soul. How would you like to have all *that* on your conscience?

But Peter's story didn't end there. Neither does yours.

Fast-forward to Resurrection Sunday. When some of Jesus' female followers approached the empty tomb, they were greeted by a young man clothed in white, who gave them some very specific instructions: "Go and tell his disciples, *including Peter*, that Jesus is going ahead of you to Galilee."[14]

As soon as Jesus was raised from the dead, Peter was on his mind. Jesus was genuinely concerned about Peter, and he wanted Peter to know that.

I don't know about you, but this story injects hope into my soul. Even if you have just made the worst mistake of your life, God isn't done with you! As long as you're still breathing, there's hope. Dream again.

Peter—the same Peter who had been afraid to admit his association with Jesus—now stood up and preached with a new boldness and authority.

After the Resurrection, Jesus spent 40 days with his closest disciples, proving that he was alive and talking to them about the Kingdom of God, before ascending to heaven to prepare a place for all of us.[15] His final mandate, besides "go and make disciples of all nations," was for his followers to wait for the empowerment they would need to carry out their commission. On day 41, it still wasn't clear to them exactly what that meant, but they continued to wait as instructed. Finally, day 50 ushered in the Holy Spirit and carved a path for Peter's comeback.

When the Holy Spirit settled on the disciples and the others who were with them, the manifestation (tongues of fire, mighty rushing wind, preaching the gospel in various languages) was so expressive and peculiar that onlookers assumed the disciples were drunk. Then Peter—the same Peter who had been afraid to admit his association with Jesus—stood up and preached with a new boldness and authority. The result was 3,000 converts and the birth of the church.[16] How's that for the result of a 41?

Wake Up!

When the Israelites trusted in the power of God, they had a long-standing history of overcoming their enemies. But they often forgot. When Goliath threatened their safety, nobody stepped forward until David showed up. If Jesse had not sent David to visit his brothers, the situation at the front would have gone downhill fast. David showed up to deliver a meal, but he ended up delivering victory to an entire nation.

The Israelites needed to wake up and become aware of what the Philistines were about to do to them. Goliath woke up David. Are you awake?

In the book of Revelation, John records a series of warnings to the churches in Asia Minor, including this message to the church in Sardis:

These are the words of him who holds the seven spirits of God and the seven stars. I know your deeds; you have a reputation of being alive, but you are dead.

Wake up! Strengthen what remains and is about to die, for I have found your deeds unfinished in the sight of my God. Remember, therefore, what you have received and heard; hold it fast, and repent. But if you do not wake up, I will come like a thief, and you will not know at what time I will come to you.[17]

Wake up. Be aware. Stay alert. Keep watch.

Pay attention to what the enemy is trying to do to your kids, your marriage, and your family. Be alert to what the enemy wants to do to your ministry. Make plans now to thwart the devil's plans to squash your dream. Guard your heart. Guard your mind. Guard your mouth. Guard your motives.

Stand Firm!

We need to wake up and be alert so we can continue to stand firm. This is easier said than done when we face a plethora of problems. David stood firm. He didn't bend to the naysayers. He didn't break under the threats of the opposition. The army of Israel was not standing firm. They had weak, wobbly knees. Not David. He stood up to Goliath and stood his ground.

Be Strong!

David was also strong in his faith. In fact, this trait is a difference maker and a game changer. The stronger we are in our faith, the stronger we will be in the face of adversity.

If we don't stand strong, we will fall—fast. It is imperative that we *believe* we can win. Peter tells us to "keep a firm grip on the faith."[18] David's grip was like a vise. Why? Because he heard God's voice over the voice of the enemy.

There is a psalm that says, "Be still, and know that I am God!"[19] This imperative is given to us in contrast to mountain-crumbling earthquakes, the "roar and foam" of the oceans, the chaos of crumbling kingdoms, and the thunder of God's voice.[20] It encourages the cultivation of an inner tranquility that allows us to hear God speaking to us even when we have a giant screaming at us.

Orfield Laboratories, a research lab in Minneapolis, features an anechoic (soundproof) chamber with background noise readings at −9.4 decibels. (That's even less sound than I hear without my hearing aids!) The chamber has double walls consisting of insulated steel, concrete, and three-foot-thick fiberglass acoustic wedges. Many businesses have rented the space to test and refine their products. Harley-Davidson used the room to develop ways to make their motorcycles quieter; NASA used the lab to train astronauts; Whirlpool and Black & Decker used it to find ways to muffle their machinery; and Cessna used the space to help produce quieter engines.

Steven Orfield, founder of Orfield Laboratories, says that the chamber "is the one place where what you hear is my actual voice."[21] It's also possible to hear "one's own heart, stomach and even inner ear, or the sounds emitted by a cellphone's display."[22]

For years, Orfield Labs held the Guinness world record as the quietest place on earth until that distinction was superseded in October 2015 by a brand-new anechoic chamber at Microsoft's headquarters in Redmond, Washington,

If you are still enough to listen to God, you will hear him say, "I've got your back."

which achieved "an average background noise reading of an unimaginably quiet −20.35 dBA.[23]

David didn't have to rent a soundproof chamber to hear God. And you don't either. If you are still enough to listen to God, you will hear him say, "I've got your back."

The apostle Paul says that faith comes by continually hearing the Word of God.[24] If you want to hear God's voice, read the Word, study the Word, feed yourself on the Word, and go to church and hear the Word proclaimed. If you struggle to comprehend God's Word, find a translation that you can understand, such as the New Living Translation (or a paraphrase such as *The Message*). If you have a difficult time reading the Bible, download the free Bible app called YouVersion, choose your Bible plan, click "Listen," and let the app read the Word to you.

If the only time you hear the Word of God is while attending a church service, your understanding and faith will never be as strong as they could be. Paul doesn't say, "Faith comes by what you heard that one time." He says that faith comes by what you *are hearing*. Paul also wrote to his protégé Timothy, "Be diligent to present yourself approved to God, a worker who does not need to be ashamed, rightly dividing the word of truth."[25]

You're Not Alone

Another way to keep a firm grip on your faith is to become aware that you are not alone in the battle. Peter writes, "You're not the only ones plunged into these hard times. It's the same with Christians all over the world."[26] The enemy wants you to believe the lie that you are all alone. This is how he gets us to isolate ourselves. He wants you to believe that you're the only one going through the storm, the wilderness, or the desert, and that you are helpless and utterly alone. It's in those moments of despair and loneliness that we feel as if no one could ever relate to our situation, so we quietly raise the white flag and accept defeat.

I am grateful for those people in my life who have encouraged me by saying, "Listen to me, dude! I made it! You're going to make it too!" That's why the writer of Hebrews commands us not to get out of the habit of meeting together for worship.[27] We need one another. We need encouragement. We need to know we're not alone. Don't get out of the habit of going to church. Instead, "keep on encouraging each other, especially since you know that the day of the Lord's coming is getting closer."[28] And Jude advises: "Build each other up in your most holy faith."[29]

Your faith will be increased by hearing the Word of God and by interacting with like-minded believers. You're not alone. We're in this together.

IT'S TIME TO RESPOND

No matter what we call the barriers we face (giant, Goliath, bully, obstacle, challenge), we all encounter some form of resistance. But how will we respond—as the army of Israel did (silence, fear, inaction) or as David did (faith, fortitude, action)?

I was in Arizona recently to speak at a youth camp, and I had the opportunity to hang out on Lynx Lake in Prescott. My friend Cory (RockChurch's student pastor) doesn't swim, but we were able to get him into the boat with us. He soon realized that was a mistake when we began playing chicken with the other boaters.

"Don't rock the boat, man! Don't rock the boat!" he screamed as my two friends and I laughed devilishly.

The army of Israel didn't want to rock the boat. Why?

Fear.

David was ready to sling a rock and bring down a giant. Why?

Faith.

The army of Israel was complacent and apathetic.

David was confident and courageous.

The army of Israel was intimidated by the enemy.

David was motivated by the enemy.

The army of Israel considered the giant's taunt a setback.

David considered it a catalyst.

David's response reminds me of an inspirational message I once heard at a conference from evangelist Tim Storey: "When you have a setback, don't take a step back. God has already prepared your comeback."

Identify your giant and be aware of your enemy's strategies. Is your giant a habit or addiction? Is it your past? It could be a financial obstacle, physical burden, or maybe the feeling of inadequacy. Regardless, it's time to let the voice of God's Word drown out the voice of your enemy.

Listen with ears of faith. Do you hear that? It's the sound of your giant dropping.

Can you hear me now?

#41WillCome
#KnowYourEnemy

TEN-FOUR, GOOD BUDDY!

David said, "What have I done now? Is there not a cause?"

1 SAMUEL 17:29, NKJV

A blind man's world is bound by the limits of his touch;
an ignorant man's world by the limits of his knowledge;
a great man's world by the limits of his vision.

AUTHOR UNKNOWN

UNLESS YOU'RE A TODDLER, older than Pez candy (invented in 1927), or you just flat-out hate technology, chances are that you own a smartphone. My wife would be the first to tell you that I allow my phone to distract me far too often. Now that I have it, I cannot imagine not having it. In fact, when I misplace my phone I feel like Gollum in *The Lord of the Rings*: "We wants it, we needs it. Must have the precious." If you don't know what that is like, you probably don't have a smartphone.

Why in the world do we love our phones so much? Because our phones can do anything except mow the grass. For example, thanks to some pretty amazing applications, my phone has the ability to do all of the following tasks: Create, receive, and send e-mails and text messages; take, edit, and upload photographs;

view, record, edit, upload, and broadcast live video; record, play, and stream music; track my steps, miles, calories, and sleeping habits; search for absolutely anything and everything on the Internet; stream television programs; purchase, store, and display books, newspapers, magazines, and PDF files; display or stream the Bible in multiple languages and translations; create content and upload blog posts; create, edit, and modify graphic design; preorder and pay for my Starbucks coffee; pay electronically when I go shopping, allowing me to leave my wallet at home (except I still need it for my driver's license); conduct banking transactions; play enough games to keep me distracted until Jesus returns; provide navigation assistance should I choose to take the next two years to walk to Alaska; communicate with my hearing aids to control volume, which especially comes in handy at the movies or when talking to a soft-spoken person (I can crank you up) or an obnoxious chatterbox (I can tone you down); and communicate with our church's security system to view live remote cameras, arm or disarm the alarm system, and even control the thermostat.

Oh, and one more thing I almost forgot: My phone also can make phone calls. (If you're old-school, you don't want anyone texting you; you want an actual phone call, right?)

Because of advances in technology, there are no excuses when it comes to our availability to communicate. If we're not on "do not disturb," we're connected 24/7/365. But it hasn't always been this way. When I was a kid, back before there were any mobile phones, the only way to communicate over a distance—apart from a landline phone or walkie-talkies—was via citizens band (CB) radio. And the only reason I wanted a CB radio when I was a kid was so I could imitate Bo and Luke Duke on *The Dukes of Hazzard*: "Shepherd to Lost Sheep, you got your ears on?" And I loved hearing Sheriff Rosco P. Coltrane sputtering to Boss Hogg: "That's a big ten-four, little fat buddy. I'm a-comin', I'm a-comin'!"

I will never forget the time my friend Trevor and I were traveling from Illinois to the Ohio church where I was the youth pastor. Trevor borrowed a CB radio so we could have some fun during our eight-hour drive. And by "fun" I mean pranking truckers. To say we ticked off some people is an understatement. I know, I know—we weren't representing Christ very well, but we were laughing so hard we were crying. (I've grown up a lot since then. Kind of.) We were having a blast until we heard the following notice go out over the airwaves: "Hey, keep your eyes open for a couple of punks in a maroon Chevy Corsica."

Busted. *Uh, that's a big ten-four!* (For the uninitiated, ten-four is CB code for "message received.")

The insulting words that Goliath hurled at Israel revealed God's plan for David. David's response was simple: *Ten-four, Big Guy in the Sky*. David knew his enemy. He was aware that God wanted him to fight the enemy, and he was willing to accept the challenge. But David's brother Eliab wasn't happy about it. "What are you doing around here anyway?" he demanded. "What about those few sheep you're supposed to be taking care of? I know about your pride and deceit. You just want to see the battle!"[1]

The question David had to ask himself was this: "Do I receive God's message or my brother's message?" He knew the answer, and thus he responded to Eliab, "What have I done now? Is there not a cause?"[2] *Embracing your cause* is the second key to holding on and standing strong until your 41 comes.

Keys to help you hold on when life gets tough and stand strong until a new day dawns

1. Know your enemy.
2. Embrace your cause.

EMBRACE YOUR CAUSE

Thanks to social media, we have no shortage of causes to engage in. If I had a dollar for every *cause* invitation I've received over the years via Facebook alone, I would be a rich man.

There are multiple categories and options to choose from (philanthropy, religion, social justice, education, medicine, environment, animals, politics). I'm amazed that there is a cause out there for just about anything and everything under the sun. In fact, as a joke—and to prove my point that people will link arms with just about any cause—I decided to create a Facebook page dedicated to the following counterfeit cause: taking the money allotted for global warming to fix shopping-cart wheels.

It doesn't matter where I shop or how many carts are available—I always end up with one that has a frenetic wheel that drags, clanks, or falls off. This must be stopped, people! Rise up, be strong, and join my "save the shopping-cart wheels" movement! Together we can make a difference. Together we can improve one's shopping experience. Together we can change the world.

Okay, that's ridiculous. It's about as ridiculous as the soldiers in Israel's army who were dressed for battle while sitting on the sidelines doing nothing. I call this *dreaming without doing*.

What about you? What's your cause? What's your dream? What's your vision? What is God asking you to do? What are the yearnings of your heart? When David later became king of Israel, he wrote a psalm that says, "Delight yourself in the LORD, and he will give you the desires of your heart."[3] Dream. Dream big. Dream so big that the only way you can ever pull it off is if God steps in. It's difficult to comprehend that God wants to launch your dreams into motion even more than you want to.

If we don't step out, will he use somebody else? Perhaps, but I don't want to find out. I used to lie in bed agonizing

Dream big. Dream so big that the only way you can ever pull it off is if God steps in.

over my dream to publish a book. My fear was that I had waited too long. And yet now you're holding my book in your hands. So my question for you right now is this: *Have you received God's message, or are you running from it?* Is it possible you're all dressed for battle but sitting on the sidelines because of some giant standing before you? Or maybe you gave up on your dream a long time ago. Well, it may be time to pick it back up, dust it off, give it to God, and let him set it into motion.

YOU ARE SOMEBODY

Have you ever witnessed an injustice and thought to yourself, *Why doesn't somebody do something?*

News flash: You *are* somebody.

When David arrived in the valley of Elah, he found a bunch of soldiers—including three of his own brothers and Saul, the king of Israel—sitting in fear of the giant, Goliath, and muttering, "Somebody should do something."

If David hadn't stepped forward to slay Goliath—if he hadn't embraced his cause—it is likely that the Israelites would have lived in bondage under the Philistines. Nobody else was answering the call. Nobody else was doing anything. While they all sat on the sidelines, David got in the game. He responded in faith and did something.

The apostle Paul tells us in Ephesians that we are God's masterpiece, "his workmanship, created in Christ Jesus for good works, which God prepared beforehand, that we should walk in them."[4]

The bottom line is that God has prepared all sorts of good works for you to do, and he wants to use you even more than you desire to be used. His plans are good plans, faith-building plans, Kingdom-establishing plans.

Just the other day, I met with an older couple who are getting married soon. Theresa told me that her fiancé, Bill, is her 41. After several failed relationships and years of abuse and heartache, she longed for God to send her a godly man. She prayed that 41 would come, and in time it did. As we sat in our meeting room at the church, Theresa's soon-to-be husband looked at me and said, "You were the first person in Theresa's life to ever tell her she's not a mistake."

Wow.

If you're feeling rejected, or as if you're in this world by accident, here's something to keep in mind: God is the one who created you, who fashioned you in your mother's womb. He saw you before your parents ever met. This means you're not an accident. You're not a mistake. God has a tailor-made plan for your life: "If people can't see what God is doing, they stumble all over themselves; but when they attend to what he reveals, they are most blessed."[5]

Do you want to be blessed? Of course! Find out what God wants you to do and do it! Because David was obedient, he was blessed. Because David was obedient, the nation of Israel was blessed. Think about that for a moment. David's willingness to accept and carry out God's plan ushered in victory not only for himself, but also for an entire nation.

> You're not an accident. You're not a mistake. God has a tailor-made plan for your life.

Helen Keller reportedly was once asked, "What could be worse than being blind?"

"Having sight without vision," she replied.

The soldiers of Israel were blinded by their fear. They

didn't see themselves as victorious. David had vision. Through his faith in God, he saw the outcome.

CALLED TO BE GREAT

Don Grosvenor, my childhood pastor and mentor, has been pastoring the same church in Phoenix, Arizona, for 55 years. As someone who has led the same church for 17 years, I find this absolutely remarkable. You have to be *called* to pastor for that long. Pastoring is messy. It's lonely. It's challenging. But if you're called by God, and you stick it out, it's rewarding, fulfilling, and life changing. Pastor Don is a role model whose faithful example and legacy have extended his reach across Phoenix and beyond.

A few weeks ago, I had the opportunity to walk through Phoenix Christian Assembly's library (aka the Hall of Fame). The rooms and walls are filled with framed photographs of ministers, missionaries, musicians, celebrities, TV personalities, and politicians whose lives have been affected over the years by the ministry of Pastor Don and Phoenix Christian Assembly. I couldn't help but think of the impact Pastor Don has had on so many for so long, all because he *received* God's message to step out in faith and *responded* by planting a church.

God has called you to be great—not just good, but great. A cheeseburger from McDonald's is good. A cheeseburger from In-N-Out Burger is great! Good teams win games. Great teams win championships. Before I planted our church, a consultant said, "Chuck, 'good enough' isn't good enough. Go build a *great* church." To do that, I need to understand what it means to be great. Jesus said, "If you want to be great, you must be the servant of all the others."[6]

Greatness is all about serving others. But too often we measure greatness by cultural standards, and we shy away because it feels prideful.

Do you desire to be great?

No. I'm humble, Chuck. I'm fine with just being okay.

Whatever.

God called David to be great. And David followed through.

It occurred to me one day that anybody in the army of Israel could have been great that day. Any one of those soldiers could have stepped up and taken out Goliath—because God was on Israel's side. It's crazy that a young teenager was the only one who *heard, listened to, embraced,* and *acted on* the message. By acting in faith, David joined a long line of faithful responders whose stories are told in the Bible.

God: Kill Goliath.
David: Ten-four.

God: I want you to sacrifice your son, Isaac.
Abraham: Ten-four. I know you will provide.

God: Build a boat in the middle of dry land even though it has never rained before.
Noah: Ten-four.

God: Rescue my people from Egypt even though they have been slaves for 400 years.
Moses (after a lot of arguing): Ten-four.

God: I want you to challenge, fight, and slaughter 850 false prophets.
Elijah: Ten-four.

God: I want you to risk your life so I can use you to save the Jews.
Esther: Ten-four.

God: Rebuild the walls of Jerusalem.
Nehemiah: Ten-four.

God: Go to Nineveh.
Jonah: Nah. [Gets swallowed by a fish and spit out on the shore.]
God: Go to Nineveh.
Jonah: Ten-four.

God: I want you to become impregnated by the Holy Spirit and give birth to the Son of God.
Mary: Ten-four.

God: Stop killing Christians and start planting churches. By the way, your name isn't Saul anymore. It's Paul.
Paul: Ten-four.

What giant is God asking you to kill? Where is God asking you to go? What do you need to rebuild? What step of faith do you need to take?

REBUILDING BROKEN WALLS

Another biblical example of someone who was stirred to action by negative news and disheartening words is Nehemiah. While living in exile in Persia, he received troubling news that rocked his world and revealed his new cause: to rebuild the walls of Jerusalem.

The report was beyond bad. It was devastating. It shook him to the core. It broke him. It left him numb. Yet Nehemiah said, "I'm going to do something about it." God backed him up, and he rebuilt the wall.

In late autumn, in the month of Kislev, in the twentieth year of King Artaxerxes' reign, I was at the fortress of Susa. Hanani, one of my brothers, came to visit me with some other men who had just arrived from Judah. I asked them about the Jews who had returned there from captivity and about how things were going in Jerusalem.

They said to me, "Things are not going well for those who returned to the province of Judah. They are in great trouble and disgrace. The wall of Jerusalem has been torn down, and the gates have been destroyed by fire."

When I heard this, I sat down and wept. In fact, for days I mourned, fasted, and prayed to the God of heaven. Then I said,

"O LORD, God of heaven, the great and awesome God who keeps his covenant of unfailing love with those who love him and obey his commands, listen to my prayer! Look down and see me praying night and day for your people Israel. I confess that we have sinned against you. Yes, even my own family and I have sinned! We have sinned terribly by not obeying the commands, decrees, and regulations that you gave us through your servant Moses.

"Please remember what you told your servant Moses: 'If you are unfaithful to me, I will scatter you among the nations. But if you return to me and obey my commands and live by them, then even if you are exiled to the ends of the earth, I will bring you back to the place I have chosen for my name to be honored.'

"The people you rescued by your great power and strong hand are your servants. O Lord, please hear my prayer! Listen to the prayers of those of us who delight in honoring you. Please grant me success today by making the king favorable to me. Put it into his heart to be kind to me."[7]

Sometimes we have to experience the ruin before we can rebuild. What in your life needs rebuilding? Family? Home? Business? Relationships? It's time to fight back! It's time to raise your voice to the enemy: "No more! I'm putting my foot down. I'm going to rebuild."

WHEN YOU LOSE EVERYTHING

A good example of someone who experienced ruin—lots of it—but chose to rebuild is my good friend John McVey. John, his wife, Julie, and their four kids attended our church, and John served on our board of elders. The McVeys were a blessed family. Julie was a stay-at-home mom and John worked for the US government. They lived in a big house on a lake, they were well respected by their peers, and their kids were all gifted and successful athletes who were heavily engrossed in their respective schools. The McVeys were involved in their community and faithful to their church.

In 2001, at age 52, John made a bad decision at work and was terminated. He didn't know it at the time, but his lapse of judgment would cost him almost everything: job, house, cars, friends, respect, and a $1.7 million pension. As John faced a web of legal ramifications and courtroom complexities, God extended grace and mercy; but John's name and reputation were smeared as his story was sensationalized in the local newspaper. To make things worse, his kids had to deal with their own consequences as they were mocked and jeered at school. For the first time in John's life, his finances were on the rocks, and his future security was uncertain.

Insert comma.

As the saying goes: Don't put a period where God puts a

comma. John's story was still being written, and it was up to him to determine how the next few chapters would turn out.

In response to this crisis, our church board rallied around John and Julie. We prayed together. We wept together. We even laughed together. In the midst of pain? Yep. In the midst of suffering? Absolutely. In the midst of failure? Of course. Happiness is based on circumstances. Joy is a choice, and we chose joy. Nehemiah says, "The joy of the LORD is your strength!"[8] It wouldn't be easy, but John and Julie chose to be strong.

I vividly remember reading Psalm 17 to them. Here's the portion I emphasized:

> I'm not trying to get my way
>   in the world's way.
> I'm trying to get *your* way,
>   your Word's way.
> I'm staying on your trail;
>   I'm putting one foot
> In front of the other.
>   I'm not giving up.[9]

John began working in the food-service industry—and when I say food-service industry, I mean fast-food industry. And when I say fast-food industry, I mean making sandwiches at Quiznos. I will never forget the time I went to visit him there; he made my sandwich, and we talked. The only part of that day I remember is that John had gone from managing 300 employees to receiving minimum wage to make sandwiches. My heart broke for him.

Please don't misunderstand me. I'm not belittling anyone in the fast-food industry or anyone who works at Quiznos. I'm sure it's a great place to work and a great place to start out, and I know there are some who have turned it into a very successful career. But at the time, I was just overwhelmed to see my good friend go from making six figures to making minimum wage. And that's not all. That particular Quiznos was a lunch hot spot in town, so John not only had to face people who knew him and his story, but he also had to make sandwiches for many employees who had worked for him at the plant he used to manage.

John worked faithfully at Quiznos for six months before landing a catering position at a local Best Western hotel. Soon after that, he was approached by the hotel owner about a business opportunity that included opening a restaurant in one of the company's vacant properties.

"I don't want my building to sit empty," the owner said, "so here's my proposition: I want to put in a Pizza Ranch franchise. I will finance the operation. You will manage and run the restaurant. You will do all the work. You will go to the Pizza Ranch franchise classes and learn their business. I will pay you a salary, and after three years you will buy me out of my original investment."

John and Julie talked and prayed about it. Then, because they didn't have the finances to hire an attorney, they agreed to the owner's terms on a handshake.

Yes! Exciting moment. Dream in motion. New chapter. Let the rebuilding begin.

John completed three weeks of intensive training at the

Pizza Ranch school, and on January 9, 2005, he opened the restaurant's doors for the first time. While grateful for the new opportunity, John was unprepared for the demands of this new business venture. Before he knew it, he was working at the restaurant 12 hours a day, seven days a week. This went on for the next three years. I remember this period well because it required us to move our monthly board meetings to the back room of the Pizza Ranch. I wasn't complaining, though, because Pizza Ranch has the best fried chicken *ever*. And their limited-edition sweet chili pizza could make a bishop kick out a stained-glass window. Yes, it was that good. *Hungry?*

Aside from putting in grueling hours, everything went fairly well for John for about eighteen months—until he received an alarming phone call from his business partner. "The numbers aren't what they need to be—and you know what that means. Owners and managers don't get paid until we're back in the black."

"Uh, that's not what we agreed to," John said. "I'll go to the bank each month and have them make out a check for what you agreed to pay me, but no more than that."

When John went to the bank the next day to conduct his normal transactions, he found that his name had been removed from the account. Access denied. Then, to complicate matters, his partner sent one of the hotel's employees to be John's new assistant manager and "keep an eye on things." In other words, as John saw it, she was a spy. Conflict and drama soon followed.

John worked under this arrangement—seven days a week, 12 hours a day, *without pay*—for more than 20 months!

Maybe right now you're thinking what I was thinking as I watched John work himself to the bone for no pay during that time: *Why put up with that? Why put yourself through it?* I knew that John was desperately trying to crawl to the three-year finish line so he could buy out his partner and no longer have to answer to him.

> **God always showed up at just the right time to keep them moving forward.**

John later told me that he stuck it out only because God sent a stranger into the restaurant to tell him: "You need to keep doing this. God is in this. Everything is going to work out."

A flicker of hope. But they weren't out of the woods yet. With the loss of income, Julie was forced to give up her stay-at-home-mom status and began putting in 65 to 70 hours each week, working two jobs for minimum wage while John toiled at the Pizza Ranch for free.

More than once, John was ready to quit, and Julie questioned God; but God always showed up at just the right time to keep them moving forward. Up and down the emotional roller coaster they went—with John's partner periodically threatening to negate their original handshake agreement.

Flummoxed, fried, and fed up by August 2007, John cried out to God from a place of desperation and devastation: "I can't do this anymore. You gotta show up with an answer, or I'm out."

Two days later, a thirtysomething man whom John had never seen before (or since) walked through the restaurant doors. His mannerisms made John uncomfortable. Finally, he approached John behind the cash register and asked, "You're a God-fearing man, aren't you?"

"Yes, I am," John answered matter-of-factly.

The man then pointed his bony finger at John and said, "This place is going to be yours. Don't worry about anything. Keep doing what you're doing. Everything that has been taken from you will be restored."

The very next day, John's partner called him and said, "I want to sell. Go to the bank and get the money."

The amount the McVeys had to come up with to purchase the franchise from John's partner was $100,000. The building was not part of the transaction. Compared to a typical business loan or franchise buy-in fee, it was not a lot of money; but it was a huge sum for John and Julie, who had no equity, no savings, and only two minimum-wage jobs as sources of income. Still, they were ecstatic at the opportunity to purchase the business and finally have some measure of control over their circumstances.

Have you ever had someone try to steal your dream? . . . Let me remind you that with God there is always hope. Trust him.

John filled out the loan application with giddy anticipation, but the answer from the loan officer was a resounding *no*. The second bank's response was the same. After six banks and six rejections, John's partner threatened to sell the business to someone else.

Have you ever had someone try to steal your dream? Perhaps you're there right now. Let me remind you that with God there is always hope. Trust him.

The McVeys consulted with a family friend who was a certified public accountant. He graciously helped them boost their financial portfolio. With renewed optimism, they approached another bank. Again they were rejected.

"I know God is on the throne," John said to me afterward, "but I'm thinking maybe he got kicked off at some point. I'm not being sacrilegious. Just keeping it real."

As we talked, John acknowledged his belief that God is never late and that his timing is always perfect. It's just hard to acknowledge this when your back is against the wall.

When John and Julie met with their CPA friend a second time, he asked John point-blank, "Why do you want to do this?"

"Because it's a God thing," John quietly responded, "and I know he's in it."

What their friend said next caught them completely off guard.

"I'm going to do the stupidest thing I've ever done in my life. I'm going to cosign the note for you."

On that amazing day in 2008 when John signed the business loan, he had less than 40 dollars in the bank.

But the story doesn't end there. When the McVeys took over the business, they incurred the restaurant's outstanding debt as well, so their financial struggles and woes continued. They began to rob Peter to pay Paul—or more precisely, to pay Uncle Sam. There was a valid concern that they would have to shut down the restaurant if they couldn't come up with the tax money. From behind the counter they would smile and say, "Welcome to Pizza Ranch," but behind their smiles were fear and frustration. John and Julie were so physically drained, emotionally overwhelmed, and mentally distraught that they could barely move forward. Have you ever cried so much that you can't cry anymore? That's where they were.

The Pizza Ranch corporation—which is Christian-owned, I should add—sent someone with financial prowess to help the McVeys for the next 18 months with stewardship, budgeting, and even tax preparation. They restructured absolutely everything. This was the equivalent of Aaron and Hur holding up the arms of Moses so Israel could win the battle.[10]

It wasn't too much longer before God prompted John to resume his giving. "It's time to give back. I want you to give back."

Three months later, John surrendered his will when he felt impressed to give a specific amount of cash to a man eating in the restaurant. After a short argument with God, John approached the booth and said, "God told me to give this to you."

Tears followed, and the man said, "My wife and I had only $18 left, and we had no idea what we were going to do."

Obedience in action.

As time went on, John continued to give money to random patrons as he felt led to, and Pizza Ranch got involved in the community. This prompted the McVeys' daughter, Selena, to suggest that they post the following message on their outdoor marquee: *Serving God in our community. How can we help you today?* People responded to the sign, and John and Julie obliged by pouring out whatever God told them to. When the fiscal year ended, John saw that sales had increased by almost 28 percent. He told me that the only thing they had done differently that year was to start listening. "And we started obeying," he said.

After some strategic planning and preparation, the McVeys decided not to renew their building lease when it expired. Instead, they purchased some land and constructed a brand-new Pizza Ranch building. They have seen their revenue more than double since they opened the doors on the new building in early 2015, and they recently opened a second franchise in another city.

After giving me permission to share their story, Julie called excitedly one day to tell me that, from the day they began their partnership with the original owner until the time they bought him out, exactly 41 months had gone by. #41WillCome #DontQuit #LiveYourDream

CULTIVATING A VISION

Before God ever gave Annette and me the vision to plant a church, we worked for a national youth ministry in Tulsa, Oklahoma, called Eastman Curtis Ministries. ECM produced a national television and radio show, operated a two-year internship program, and hosted regional youth conventions across the United States and Canada. While living in Tulsa, I attended and served at Church on the Move and Guts Church. Each Sunday night at the edgy and contemporary Guts service, I thought to myself how cool something like that would be in central Illinois. I didn't have a desire to do it. I just thought it would be cool if somebody did. Yeah, I ended up being that somebody.

On my way home from a youth convention in Canada at three o'clock in the morning, I was driving our ministry van while rocking out to some Danny Chambers worship music. It was in that moment that I thought about the statistics of people leaving the church in droves. I thought about how desperately central Illinois needed a Guts-type church. I was tired of hearing about friends back home who were quitting church and giving up on God. It was also in that moment that I clearly heard God ask me to be the one to do something about it. My response was simple and immediate: "You got it, God. I'm in. Ten-four. Roger that."

Be aware of your enemy. *Done.*

Embrace your cause. *Done.*

Now what?

One of my favorite passages in Scripture regarding vision is found in the Old Testament book of Habakkuk:

The LORD said to me,
"Write my answer plainly on tablets,
    so that a runner can carry the correct message to
       others.
This vision is for a future time.
    It describes the end, and it will be fulfilled.
If it seems slow in coming, wait patiently,
    for it will surely take place.
    It will not be delayed."[11]

There are three takeaways about vision that I want to hammer home from this passage:

1. Write it down.
2. Run with it.
3. Wait for it.

Write It Down

One way to begin to bring your vision to life is to write it down. Habakkuk says to make it plain on *tablets*, so grab your iPad or Galaxy and throw it down, right? Yes! I believe something remarkable happens when we write down our vision. It's almost as if we ignite some subliminal accountability. Something comes alive, as if we are flipping a switch or lighting a match.

Do you have a goal? A cause? A vision? A dream? Write it down. Type it out. Record it in a journal.

> Do you have a goal? A cause? A vision? A dream? Write it down. Type it out. Record it in a journal.

Not long after my burning-bush experience in that ministry van somewhere between the Canadian border and Tulsa, I wrote down my vision to plant a church. Annette and I wrote down our goals. We detailed the vision and shared it with family and friends. We covered it in prayer. We wrote down specific attendance goals for our first service and our second service, and we wrote down where we wanted to be after one year and five years. We documented everything we could think of, printed it out, put it in a binder, and began praying consistently about it.

A recent study at Dominican University confirms that writing down your goals increases your chances of accomplishing them. In fact, their study showed that up to 76 percent of those who wrote down their goals, shared them with a friend, and established weekly accountability had either accomplished their goals or were well on their way.[12]

Pro football Hall of Famer Emmitt Smith—yes, the same Emmitt Smith who won *Dancing with the Stars*—attributes his success in part to the practice he developed early in life of writing down his goals. Check out what he said, right after he acknowledged Jesus Christ, during his Hall of Fame induction speech in 2010:

> I wrote down my goals and how I was going to achieve them because Dwight Thomas [Smith's high school football coach] used to tell us, "It's only a dream until you write it down, and then it becomes a goal." By the time I was 20, I wrote, I want to play in the Super Bowl, be the MVP, become the all-time leading rusher, and finish college, because I promised my mother I would.
>
> Over the course of my career, all of those things came to pass, and I know that writing down my goals was an essential strategy.[13]

That is certified boom sauce, people! And it originated in Scripture.

Run with It

Writing down your vision causes it to grow wings and pre-pares it for liftoff. Writing down Annette's and my vision to plant RockChurch caused others to pick it up and run with it alongside us. As we continued to communicate our vision on a regular basis, everyone on our launch team began to pick it up, embrace it, and run with it. It was big-ger than Annette and me. It was bigger than our family. It was more than *my* vision. It became *their* vision. Now it's *our* vision, and more than 17 years later, we're all still run-ning with it.

As you write down, pick up, and run with your vision, it's vital to surround yourself with people who believe in you, people who are going to encourage you, people who will block for you so that, like Emmitt Smith, you can run with it into the end zone.

Wait on It

Notice that Habakkuk tells us to wait patiently for our vision—even if it seems slow in coming. It might take some time, but if it's God's plan and we're obedient to him, it will happen. Don't quit. We must keep our eyes on the goal and keep running. We must keep moving. As soon as we stop, we become stagnant.

Don't get complacent. Don't get discouraged. Embrace your cause. Write it down. Run with it. Keep running. Keep waiting.

Proverbs 24:10 says that if we quit when times are tough, if we quit in times of adversity, our strength is small. Too many people allow their problems to knock them out of the race when their victory is right around the corner. Don't do that! Be patient. Keep running. Keep fighting.

Leadership developer John C. Maxwell writes, "Vision has power because it provides leaders with awareness—the ability to see . . . attitude—the faith to believe . . . [and] action—the courage to do."[14]

Come on, let's go be brave!

#41WillCome
#EmbraceYourCause

SMASHMOUTH

As soon as the Israelite army saw him, they began to run away in fright. "Have you seen the giant?" the men asked.

1 SAMUEL 17:24-25, NLT

Courage is resistance to fear, mastery of fear—not absence of fear.

MARK TWAIN, *PUDD'NHEAD WILSON*

MOST FEARS AREN'T RATIONAL. Remember that.

As soon as you embrace your vision and decide that you're going to launch your dreams into motion, the enemy will use anything and everything to immobilize you with fear. Fear can stop you in your tracks. Fear can be crippling. It takes only the slightest bit of fear to crush your faith and derail your dreams.

What prevented the army of Israel from accepting Goliath's challenge?

What stopped the soldiers from defending the honor of the God they served?

What terminated their dream of conquering the Philistines and winning the hand of King Saul's daughter in marriage?

What quashed every soldier's vision of killing the giant and being hoisted onto the shoulders of his fellow soldiers for a victory parade through the streets of Israel?

Fear.

Let's break down 1 Samuel 17:24: "As soon as the Israelite army saw him [Goliath], they began to run away in fright."[1]

Israel was God's chosen nation. They were his people. He had called them to greatness. They were dressed for battle and backed by the Creator of the universe, but they weren't doing anything . . . because they were afraid. They simply sat on the sidelines, dejected and intimidated.

Fear can talk us out of anything, but it doesn't have to. That's where faith and courage come in.

From a strictly human perspective, their fear was understandable. Goliath was one big dude. And he was mean, to boot. So when they saw the giant, "they began to run away in fright." That's what I would have done. That's probably what you would have done. That's what we'd all do.

"Have you seen the giant?" When it comes down to fight or flight and there's a giant involved, flight is the sane and rational play. Fear can talk us out of anything, but it doesn't have to. That's where faith and courage come in.

COURAGE

It takes courage to kill giants and deliver dreams. Courage is the quality of mind or spirit that enables a person to face difficulty, danger, pain, giants, and mountains. In the words of Pudd'nhead Wilson, the title character in a Mark Twain story, "Courage is resistance to fear, mastery of fear—not absence of fear."[2]

Courage doesn't mean you're not afraid. Courage means that, in spite of your fear, you're going to step out and face the challenge anyway. Courage means you're going to smash fear in the mouth, pin it to the ground, and force it to tap out!

This is the third key to help you hold on and stand strong until your 41 comes: *Smash fear in the mouth.*

Keys to help you hold on when life gets tough and stand strong until a new day dawns

1. *Know your enemy.*
2. *Embrace your cause.*
3. *Smash fear in the mouth.*

David smashed fear in the mouth by displaying immeasurable courage. But that doesn't mean he wasn't afraid when he went out to fight Goliath. He simply did what nobody else would do—he stepped onto the battlefield, willing to take on the impossible.

If fear is a deal breaker, courage is the difference maker. It was David's faith in God that ultimately gave him the confidence and courage to grab five smooth stones and declare, "I'm going to take this giant out!"

PHOBIAS

I used to have a dachshund named Buster. Buster was the coolest wiener dog ever. He loved everybody. And he especially loved company. He would completely lose his mind every time someone came to the door.

Ding-dong . . . zip! Like a NASCAR driver on Red Bull, Buster would be turning circles at the front door. The only problem was that he would get so excited that he was unable to control his bladder. If anyone reached down to pet him, he would collapse onto his side and start squirting like a water gun. But that's a story for another time.

The thing about Buster, and part of what made him so cool, was that he was fearless of big dogs. I don't care if you had a pit bull, boxer, Doberman, or Rottweiler, Buster would go on the attack. But if a fly got into the house, he would tuck tail and run under the bed. That's *pteronarcophobia*, the fear of flies. I guess we all have our Achilles' heel. (#SmashFear)

What are you afraid of? What's holding you back? What is absolutely freaking you out right now? What is the devil using to intimidate you? We all have phobias. We all have irrational fears. For example, if you throw a snake at me, I'm gone! I hate snakes. The only kind of snakes I can tolerate are dead ones or the ones secured behind glass.

I read about a guy who was trying to impress his girlfriend, so he pulled his pet rattlesnake out of its cage, and it bit him on the neck! (You can't make this stuff up.) I also viewed a recent Instagram thread about a guy who plays with cobras. One picture featured him lying in a hospital bed giving a thumbs-up sign, apparently after being bit on the abdomen.

Here's a little tip: If you own a venomous snake, keep it in its cage! Let me remind you that, out of every animal on the planet, the devil chose to inhabit a snake in the Garden of Eden.

One my best friends, Jason, has *arachnophobia*. He is deathly afraid of spiders, which has led to several pranks over the years. And I've had my own run-ins with our eight-legged enemies—like the time I was performing an outdoor wedding under a gazebo and almost jumped out of my clothes when a groomsman approached me slowly and said, "Don't move. There's a spider . . ."

And what happens to nine out of ten people when they walk through a spiderweb? They start flailing about like they're insane. And of course, no one else can see the spiderweb. They just assume you're nuts.

Ecclesiophobia is the fear of church . . . which is one reason I planted RockChurch. Our mission has always been to reach people who don't feel comfortable in a traditional church setting. If you're one of them, please don't allow a bad experience at a church to keep you from an authentic, growing relationship with Jesus Christ.

As long as we're on the topic of phobias, I'll confess to another one of mine: *aviophobia*, the fear of flying. I have flown countless times—all over the US, plus to Africa, Europe, Mexico, and Jamaica—but I still get nervous every time. Not sometimes—*every single time.*

I'm the guy with the sweaty palms, quoting Psalm 91 under his breath.

> This I declare about the LORD:
> He alone is my refuge, my place of safety;
>   he is my God, and I trust him. . . .
>
> He will cover you with his feathers.
>   He will shelter you with his wings.
> His faithful promises are your armor and
>   protection. . . .
> He will order his angels
>   to protect you wherever you go.[3]

There was one instance when we hit some turbulent air, and our flight attendant started buckling in, looking completely terrified. When I saw the fear on her face, I almost passed out! I was thinking, *Okay, this lady's job is to comfort people like me. If* she's *freaked out, then what the heck is really going on?*

So yes, I'm afraid when I fly, but here's the deal: My fear of flying doesn't stop me from doing it. I conquer my aviophobia every time I climb aboard a plane.

Do you remember the first time you rode a roller coaster? If your answer is, "No, you'll never get me on a roller coaster," you may have *coaster phobia*. Some people call it *veloxrotaphobia*, which translates to "fear of quick wheels," but no one can actually pronounce it—hence, coaster phobia.

The first roller coaster I ever went on was called the Demon Drop. It was two loops sandwiched between all kinds of scary. Was I scared? Yes—terrified. Did I go back on it again? You bet. My fear was irrational. I would have missed out on so much fun that day if I hadn't conquered my joint fears of riding a roller coaster *and* going upside down.

This reminds me of a story . . . because everything reminds me of a story.

I lived in Sandusky, Ohio, for about two years while youth pastoring at a small Assemblies of God church in Bellevue. If you like roller coasters, you know that the best amusement park in the world is Cedar Point. (If you disagree, you're wrong.) It's called "America's Roller Coast" for two reasons: (1) It overlooks Lake Erie, and (2) it has more roller coasters than any other park. Cedar Point always has the world's tallest or fastest ride. The word *awesome* doesn't do it justice.

When my little sister and I were teenagers, her very first roller coaster experience involved me and the Magnum XL-200, which at the time was the world's tallest and fastest steel coaster. I had somehow talked Cherie into riding it by saying something like "Don't worry. It's not too scary."

I lied.

Cherie was afraid of heights and had never been on a roller coaster in her life. After waiting in line for what seemed like eight days, it was finally our turn to climb aboard. It's easy to be brave while standing in line, but when the moment of truth arrives, a lot of people chicken out. That would be my sister. That's right, when it came time to climb aboard, she changed her mind. (Have you done that before?)

I pleaded with her, "No! Come on, Cherie, you can do this!"

All the color in her face disappeared and she responded adamantly, "No way, Chuck. I'm too scared!"

I knew I had to think fast or she was going to miss out on the greatest experience of her life. I stared into her eyes and said as convincingly as I could, "Well, hey, it's okay, because here's the deal. Each car has a button, so while we're making our ascent, if you get too frightened, just push the button and they will stop the ride to let you off."

I know. I'm a bad brother.

I must have convinced her, because she quietly said, "Okay." We hopped on board and buckled in. (By the way, just so you know, I did end up repenting for this. God has already forgiven me for what happened next.)

The ride began its clickety-clank ascent to the top. (If you want to get a sense of just how long that is, you can check out the YouTube video.) We were going up and up and up!

Clickety-clank. Clickety-clank. Clickety-clank.

Two weeks later, the Magnum reached its highest point. The view (for me) was breathtaking, as Lake Erie majestically appeared ahead and to the right. Of course, Cherie was missing the view because she had her head buried between her legs while maintaining a death grip on the safety bar in front of her. It looked like she was trying to crawl down on the floor of the car.

As we were about to arrive at the top, I tapped her back and called her name.

No response.

I hollered a little louder, "Cherie! Cherie!"

Nothing.

Finally, I yelled, "Cherie! Do you want me to push the button?"

She looked up and shrieked, "Yes!"

That's when, unfortunately for her, I laughed mischievously.

"Sorry! There is no button!"

Vrooooooooooooooooom! Down the drop we went.

Yes, I'm a horrible person. After about six weeks of therapy she started talking again. (Kidding.) She ribbed me recently after I used this story as a sermon illustration. I quickly pointed out that I had actually helped her overcome her fears, as she is no longer afraid of roller coasters. Then I added, "You're welcome."

FAILURE

You may not be fraught with the fears I've mentioned thus far. Let's face it, a fear of spiders isn't going to prevent you from accomplishing what God has predestined you to do. Being afraid to jump from a cliff into a river is not going to determine whether your dream to design video games comes to fruition. Your fear of sharks will not stop your pursuit of becoming a physician, architect, entrepreneur, or pizza-franchise owner. So let's talk about a big, valid fear that confronts *everyone*. I'm talking about the fear of failure.

> The fear of failure attacks us from two separate angles: being afraid to *begin* . . . and being afraid to *begin again.*

The fear of failure attacks us from two separate angles:

being afraid to *begin* (because we're afraid of failing) and being afraid to *begin again* (because we failed the last time). I believe that the devil uses our fear of failure to dash more dreams than any other phobia out there. This phobia defeats us before we even begin and pummels us after we fail.

When I was a teenager, I experienced a sudden onset of fear after climbing the ladder of a high dive. Now, I *love* diving boards, and I even won a gold medal way back in the day . . . at youth camp. I was always up for trying new tricks: full gainer; half gainer; backflip; backward one-and-a-half; frontward one-and-a-half; front flip with a half twist that ends in a can-opener; and the ever-popular backward butt-buster—which is where you free-fall backward to land with your bottom on the diving board, launching yourself into a backflip ending in a can-opener. (A word of caution: The butt-buster will get you kicked out of a public pool.)

The only thing I was afraid to try was a frontward two-and-a-half from a high dive. I thought about it every summer until I finally mustered enough courage to make an attempt. I wish I could tell you that I was successful. But my attempt at the two-and-a-half flip from the high dive turned out more like a very successful two-and-a-belly-flop. *Spin. Spin. Smack! Ouch! Chuck, you're an idiot.* I spent the rest of the day on the pool deck watching everyone else. Luckily for me, YouTube didn't exist back then or my dive would now be showcased on "Epic Fails." I never did try it again. But do I think about it? Yep. Am I glad I gave it a shot? Absolutely. I would rather fail while trying than think about *what-if*s for the rest of my life. Will I try it again? There's still time.

Fear of failure almost prevented Moses from receiving a second chance. After he had committed murder and hidden in the desert for 40 years, he was commissioned by God via burning bush to be the rescuer of Israel. Failure has a way of gnawing at us so much that we start to believe we can never be used by God . . . even when God is the one asking us to do something. In Moses' case, instead of accepting the epic opportunity that God was presenting, he began to argue based on his self-perceived flaws and insecurities.

"What if they won't believe me or listen to me? What if they say, 'The LORD never appeared to you'?"

Then the LORD asked him, "What is that in your hand?"

"A shepherd's staff," Moses replied.

"Throw it down on the ground," the LORD told him. So Moses threw down the staff, and it turned into a snake! Moses jumped back.

Then the LORD told him, "Reach out and grab its tail." So Moses reached out and grabbed it, and it turned back into a shepherd's staff in his hand.

"Perform this sign," the LORD told him. "Then they will believe that the LORD, the God of their ancestors—the God of Abraham, the God of Isaac, and the God of Jacob—really has appeared to you."

Then the LORD said to Moses, "Now put your hand inside your cloak." So Moses put his hand inside his cloak, and when he took it out again, his hand was white as snow with a severe skin disease.

"Now put your hand back into your cloak," the
Lord said. So Moses put his hand back in, and when
he took it out again, it was as healthy as the rest of
his body.

The Lord said to Moses, "If they do not believe
you and are not convinced by the first miraculous
sign, they will be convinced by the second sign. And
if they don't believe you or listen to you even after
these two signs, then take some water from the Nile
River and pour it out on the dry ground. When you
do, the water from the Nile will turn to blood on the
ground."

But Moses pleaded with the Lord, "O Lord, I'm
not very good with words. I never have been, and
I'm not now, even though you have spoken to me. I
get tongue-tied, and my words get tangled."

Then the Lord asked Moses, "Who makes a
person's mouth? Who decides whether people speak
or do not speak, hear or do not hear, see or do not
see? Is it not I, the Lord? Now go! I will be with you
as you speak, and I will instruct you in what to say."

But Moses again pleaded, "Lord, please! Send
anyone else."

Then the Lord became angry with Moses. "All
right," he said. "What about your brother, Aaron
the Levite? I know he speaks well. And look! He is
on his way to meet you now. He will be delighted
to see you. Talk to him, and put the words in his
mouth. I will be with both of you as you speak, and

I will instruct you both in what to do. Aaron will be your spokesman to the people. He will be your mouthpiece, and you will stand in the place of God for him, telling him what to say. And take your shepherd's staff with you, and use it to perform the miraculous signs I have shown you."[4]

If God calls you, that's good enough. We're all flawed, we all have insecurities, and we all occasionally magnify our personal propensities—which is why I'm so glad that God doesn't use perfect people. The 66 books that make up the Bible contain more than 31,000 verses filled with *ordinary* people—people like you and me—who ended up doing *extraordinary* things. The following is a list of several Bible heroes who failed, and yet God still performed exploits through them.

- **Noah:** got drunk and exposed himself
- **Abraham:** liar, liar, pants on fire
- **Jacob:** cheater, cheater, pumpkin eater
- **Tamar:** disguised herself as a prostitute and had sex with her father-in-law
- **Judah:** slept with his daughter-in-law and ordered her to be burned (until his own sin was exposed)
- **Moses:** committed murder and argued with God
- **Rahab:** prostitute
- **Elijah:** overcome by despair, he threw in the towel and asked God to take his life
- **David:** committed adultery and murder and lied about it

- **Jonah:** rebelled against God, freaked out a bunch of people on a boat, made a big fish really sick
- **Peter:** tried to correct Jesus, chopped off a person's ear, denied Christ three consecutive times, cussed out a little girl
- **Saul (aka Paul):** captured and murdered Christians, tried to destroy the church that Christ had started

"God puts the fallen on their feet again and pushes the wicked into the ditch."[5] David wrote those words because he had lived them over and over again.

The next time you fall on your face, instead of beating yourself up, get up and shout, "Do not gloat over me, my enemies! For though I fall, I will rise again. Though I sit in darkness, the LORD will be my light."[6]

HOT TUBS, DREAMS, AND FAILING FORWARD

My good friends Tim and Maureen Gray know what it's like to experience utter failure.

I first met Tim and Maureen while working for Eastman Curtis Ministries in Tulsa during the 1990s. Tim and I traveled the country as part of ECM's "This Generation" youth convention team. I was the convention manager, and Tim was our media broker and Eastman's right-hand man. It didn't matter which city we were in; after every two-day youth conference, Tim and I would celebrate the weekend by relaxing in the hotel hot tub. Even when it was after-hours, Tim would find a way to convince the hotel manager to let us use the hot tub, or we would somehow break in. We would discuss the wins and losses of that particular youth convention and talk about life, but mostly we would dream—and laugh—a lot. Tim dreamed about making an impact in the world through Christian media. I dreamed about planting a church for people who didn't like church.

Fast-forward several years. I was now pastoring the church in Illinois that I had dreamed of planting. Tim and Maureen were pastoring their own church plant in Tulsa, while Tim continued working for a media company on the side. After brokering media for countless churches and serving in an associate-pastor role for a handful of pastors, Tim's turn to shine had come. It was time to step out and step up. For Tim and Maureen, it was finally their time to lead and to implement what they had learned along the way.

Two and a half years later, they flat out quit.

If you've ever been involved in a church, you already know that wherever there are people, there are problems. Maybe that's why some people no longer go to church. If you're a pastor or other leader, you know firsthand how challenging the church can be. Ministry is messy.

Conflict.

Competition.

Tension.

Drama.

Strife.

Staff transition.

Theological disagreements.

Doctrinal differences.

Unrealistic expectations.

Financial pressure.

Power plays.

Frustration.

Manipulation.

Did I mention *people*?

I wouldn't be surprised to find out that the very first person ever to use the hashtag *#thestruggleisreal* was a perplexed pastor. I know—I've been there. I'm currently 17 years in, and I can't tell you how many times I've driven to the edge of town to practice leaving. Heck, I did quit once. I didn't end up following through, but I told our board I was moving back to Tulsa. We had three or four families committed to go with us. But I knew in my heart it was the wrong decision, so we backed out before we ever announced it to the congregation.

Tim and Maureen didn't practice leaving. They left.

Tim was sensitive to the fact that he couldn't effectively pastor *and* work for a media company. Thus, the decision came down to choosing between jobs. The Grays finally came to the gut-wrenching conclusion that it would be easier—and less stressful—to dissolve their church. Maureen told me that the Sunday they resigned was one of the hardest and saddest days of their lives. "The church was birthed out of a genuine calling and obedience to God," she said. "But it failed. We missed God. More than anything else over the last 20 years of our lives, this was a catastrophic failure."

After setting aside his dream and allowing the mayhem of ministry to get the best of him, Tim was eager to go full-time with the company he had spent the previous 10 years helping to build. Forty-eight hours later, he was fired.

Yes, you read that right. Resigned from church on Sunday. Fired from job on Tuesday.

Ouch. Double whammy.

Have I mentioned that the Grays have six children?

How do you slay the giant when you're permeated with absolute despair? What do you do after you've laid down your dreams and ended up with nothing? You trust God.

> **What do you do after you've laid down your dreams and ended up with nothing? You trust God.**

That's easier said than done. As Maureen admitted, "Over the next two months, I didn't know how to hear God anymore. Tim and I were no longer praying out of purpose; I was praying out of desperation. I cried out constantly for God to help us. We lost sight of God's goodness. We were no longer resting in his peace."

Still, they kept praying—even as they sold everything they owned just to survive and were forced to move out of their home. Then they ran out of money.

During those months of misery, the Grays almost moved to three different cities. But something fell through each time. Regardless, their kids were not going to be able to go back to the private school they had always attended. Their eldest, in college at the time, would not be able to go back for her sophomore year.

But God had not forsaken them.

During this time of desperation and praying, it just so happened that they received a check in the mail, out of the blue, from a friend who was unaware of their plight. The attached note read: "God is with you. Nothing broken. Nothing missing." The amount of the check was the exact amount they needed to enroll their kids in school. It was as if God had breathed on the few remaining embers of Maureen's heart and reignited hope that he was moving behind the scenes.

"It gave us reassurance," she said, "that God was hearing us."

From that moment on, God began to provide for each day, one need at a time. Next, Tim and Maureen were approached by an acquaintance, who asked, "Do you know anybody who would want to move into a house that I can't take care of until it sells?"

Uh, yeah.

"I only need $250 per month to cover basic upkeep."

The Grays didn't even have the required $250 to move in, so they were forced to sell some more stuff and pawn some personal items. With the help of the high school football team—their daughter's friends—they packed their remaining belongings and moved into the "worst house we had ever lived in," Maureen said. "It was old, dirty, and smelly, yet I heard God say, 'This will be a place of healing and restoration . . . if you allow it to be.'"

Done. They settled in and thanked God for providing a place to live.

One week later, Maureen's sister sent her a plane ticket to visit her in Canada so that Maureen could get a short break from the insanity and catch her breath. After all, they had no income and no one as yet would hire Tim. Maureen determined that she would attempt to substitute teach and Tim could sell cars if he had to.

On the day Maureen flew to her sister's, she and Tim had only $47 to their name. Nothing in checking. Nothing in savings. Just two twenties and seven ones. Tim kept one of the twenties for himself and gave Maureen the rest. "I don't know what we're going to do," he said to her, "but God does." (#SmashFearInTheMouth)

As Maureen sat on the plane, she took out her Bible and read Psalm 34: "I prayed to the LORD, and he answered me. He freed me from all my fears."[7] She later told me, "God was doing something that I couldn't see."

We should never forget that God is always moving and that nothing ever catches him off guard or by surprise.

Tim returned home from the airport, went straight into the bedroom, and prayed like there was no tomorrow. Ninety minutes later he received a phone call out of the blue to purchase media for a pro-life campaign that was tied to a senatorial race. Tim was honest and admitted that, in all his years of selling media, he had "never done political stuff."

We should never forget that God is always moving and that nothing ever catches him off guard or by surprise.

"We don't care," they said. "Just do it."

By the time Maureen landed in Canada, Tim had brokered a deal for $47,000! *Bam! Go, God!* I am just as excited writing this as I was the first time Tim and Maureen shared this story with Annette and me. God is faithful. Every. Single. Time.

Tim brokered that memorable deal in September 2004. The financial windfall carried the Grays through the end of the year, and they launched Gray Media in January 2005.

Within one year, they paid off $100,000 in debt and began to build their company as God opened doors and bestowed his supernatural favor on them. They have since been able to pay for all six of their kids to go to college, and two of them now work for Gray Media.

Here is a list of how God has grown and blessed Gray Media since Tim's $47,000 phone call in 2004:

- Gray Media has placed media in almost every country in the world
- Tim brokered the deal for the very first religious program on E! Channel
- Gray Media is responsible for adding faith programming to USA Network
- It represents and oversees all media for T. D. Jakes
- It represents the largest church in western Europe
- It brokered media contracts for successful Christian films such as *Soul Surfer, God's Not Dead,* and *Heaven Is for Real*
- It brokered media deals for 11 Christian films during 2014 alone
- It is responsible for securing faith-based content at the Sundance Film Festival
- Gray Media now delivers faith-based content to Netflix
- It represents the most successful Hispanic pastor in the world, who oversees more than 40,000 churches in the US, with 16 million Hispanics, and more than 500,000 congregations worldwide.[8]

It's important to point out that, during the past 11 years, Tim has never brokered another political buy—not even one— since the miraculous phone call that set his dream in motion.

NOW WHAT?

It's easy for me to say, "Don't be afraid," but maybe you're thinking, *Okay, I know I can't let fear stop me, but how?*

There are two surefire ways to smash fear in the face:

1. Trust God.
2. Step out.

The first way to smash fear in the mouth is to *trust God* and believe what his Word says. If you want to refresh your spirit, go back and review the Scriptures we looked at in chapter 3:

- 1 Samuel 17:36
- Jeremiah 29:11
- Matthew 19:26
- Romans 8:9-11, 31-39
- Ephesians 2:10
- 1 John 4:4

God's got your back, as David professes in Psalm 125: "Those who trust in the LORD are as secure as Mount Zion; they will not be defeated but will endure forever."[9]

Let me throw down how some other translations handle this verse:

- **CEV:** "Everyone who trusts the LORD . . . cannot be shaken and will stand forever."
- **MSG:** "Those who trust in GOD are like Zion Mountain: Nothing can move it, a rock-solid mountain you can always depend on."
- **ESV:** "Those who trust in the LORD are like Mount Zion, which cannot be moved."
- **TLB:** "Those who trust in the Lord are steady as Mount Zion, unmoved by any circumstance."

Notice that David doesn't imply that we will never be afraid. Instead, he says that we will overcome and win . . . in spite of our fears or circumstances. (#BoomSauce)

The second way to smash fear in the mouth is to *step out*. We're going to cover this in greater detail in chapter 10, but here I at least want to point out that David had to *pick up* his slingshot and *step onto the battlefield*. Had he not stepped out, Goliath wouldn't have fallen. Faith without works is dead. You can trust God to protect you, but if you stay on the sidelines it doesn't really matter, does it? So how do you move from the sidelines to the playing field? You put one foot in front of the other. Jump. Go. Start. Flip. Fly. Fight. Get in the ring. Step onto the field. "The LORD rejoices to see the work begin."[10] Start.

If we're going to smash fear in the mouth and move forward with our dreams, then it's imperative that we wrap our hearts around the words of Paul in his second letter to Timothy: "God has not given us a spirit of fear and timidity, but of power, love, and self-discipline."[11]

If fear doesn't come from God, then whom does it come from? The very same enemy we identified in chapter 4. Not only have we identified our enemy, but we also are now aware of his schemes. This means he can no longer hamstring us with fear. We're on to his game.

David trusted God. Do you?

David stepped out. Are you ready to?

Kick fear to the curb and keep reading.

#41WillCome
#SmashFearInTheMouth

7

SHAKE IT OFF!

"Don't be ridiculous!" Saul replied. "There's no way you
can fight this Philistine and possibly win! You're only a
boy, and he's been a man of war since his youth."

1 SAMUEL 17:33, NLT

I have to remember to tell the negative committee that
meets in my head to sit down and shut up.

AUTHOR UNKNOWN

IDENTIFY MY ENEMY. *Check.*

Be aware of my enemy's schemes. *Check.*

Believe I really can defeat my enemy. *Check.*

Embrace my cause. *Check.*

Move from fear to faith by stepping onto the battlefield.
Check.

Act like Taylor Swift and *Shake It Off.*

Huh?

Keep reading.

The moment David stepped onto the battlefield, he was
slapped in the face with doubt as Goliath mocked and made
fun of him. This is not a mind-blowing revelation. We expect
skepticism and smack talk from the enemy. After all, the
unruly giant had already been talking smack to Israel for

40 consecutive days. And in chapter 9 we'll see how David delivered some smack talk of his own and then backed it up by putting the smackdown on Goliath.

You expect negativity from your haters, right? You expect to be razzed and ridiculed by your enemy. You expect smack talk from the opposing team. You expect Twitter wars between pop stars and athletes who can't stand each other. Haters gonna hate, right? You don't, however, expect it from your own team. And you most definitely don't expect it from your own family.

FAMILY, FRIENDS, AND FLATS

When David heard Goliath make his daily challenge, he inquired about the reward for anyone brave enough to fight the giant. The response from his own brother Eliab was, "Go home, dude!" In my mind, I hear Eliab mimicking and impersonating a sheep as a way to jeer David.

"Go baaaack to Daaaad! Come on, Daaaavid! Go baaaack to your sheep!"

Laughter.

It hurts to be mocked by your own siblings, doesn't it? When your own family doesn't believe in you, it cuts to the core. Perhaps you're there right now. Maybe you have finally decided to chase your dream only to be dissuaded by doubters under your own roof. Well, as my friend Todd would say, "Carry on, soldier. You got this."

That's what David did. He dismissed doubt and went straight to King Saul. But all he got for his trouble was more doubt and discouragement.

One would think that—after 40 days of cowardice from

his own soldiers—the king would be ecstatic to finally find somebody who was brave enough to step up. Nope. Instead, King Saul said, "You don't have a chance against him. . . . You're only a boy, and he's been a soldier all his life."[1]

Thanks for the vote of confidence, Your Royal Highness.

When you're driving, there's almost nothing worse than getting a flat tire. It's a horrible feeling to be on the side of the road changing a tire or waiting for somebody to come do it for you. I wish they had an app for that! Wouldn't it be great to click a "Change Tire" button and know that someone would be on their way? There's your 41 business idea—no extra charge.

I will never forget the time I had three flat tires in one week. I finally decided to quit parking on broken glass. But seriously, do you know *anyone* who has ever gotten three flats in one week? Yep, Chuck Tate! I went to a garage in the afternoon and had my tire fixed, and the next morning it was flat again. I went back to the same garage and brought the tire with me. When I walked up to the counter and told the guy, "I was here last night. You guys fixed this tire. It's flat again," he said—and I wish I were lying—"So . . . it's still leaking, huh?"

> Sharing your vision with the wrong people is like letting the air out of your own tires.

Sharing your vision with the wrong people is like letting the air out of your own tires. If David had listened to his brothers, he would have been deterred from his destiny. Here's a quick tip: Surround yourself with people who believe in you.

David could easily have crumbled, as most people would have. Who would have blamed him? In fact, everyone was probably hoping and praying he would change his mind. But David wasn't like most people. He knew that succumbing to words of doubt would derail his dream and win him a one-way ticket back to the sheepfold. So instead of listening to King Saul, he obeyed a greater King. Instead of punching a one-way ticket home, he won the keys to the kingdom. His decision to step up would eventually land him on the very throne of the king who told him he didn't belong.

I'm getting ahead of the story here, but it's important to mention that King Saul reigned as Israel's king for 40 years . . . which meant that David became king in year 41. (#41WillCome)

Saul was the people's choice. David was God's choice.

If you want to kill the giant that stands between you and your new day dawning, you need to learn the fourth key: *Shake off doubts and doubters.*

Keys to help you hold on when life gets tough and stand strong until a new day dawns

1. *Know your enemy.*
2. *Embrace your cause.*
3. *Smash fear in the mouth.*
4. *Shake off doubts and doubters.*

SHAKING OFF HATERS AND DOUBTERS

Scripture tells us that "bad company corrupts good character."[2] I think we all would agree. Another translation says,

"Bad friends will destroy you."[3] I have counseled numerous people who have experienced devastating heartache and avoidable calamity simply because of the people whom they associated with. A lot of people sitting in prison today are there because the wrong crowd led them into a hole they couldn't climb out of. You can't surround yourself with negativity and expect positive results.

What may not be quite as apparent, but is nonetheless true, is that well-meaning "good company" can also corrupt or hinder our God-given dreams. Well-meaning friends and family can often squelch what God has placed in our hearts.

So what do we do when this happens? We need to act like David and shake it off. David loved his brothers and respected King Saul, but he refused to let them talk him out of what God had put in his heart. As Joel Osteen writes, "The dream in your heart may be bigger than the environment in which you find yourself. Sometimes you have to get out of that environment in order to see that dream fulfilled."[4] For David, that meant getting off the sidelines and into the battle.

Once we are certain of where God is leading us, we need to be willing to stand our ground and shake off the doubters. I had to learn this lesson in my own life.

After I had been youth pastoring in Ohio for almost two years, God opened the door for me to join Eastman Curtis Ministries in Tulsa. ECM produced a national television program called *This Generation* on the Inspirational Network (and, later, on the Trinity Broadcasting Network), broadcast a national radio program, and hosted regional youth conventions across the United States and Canada.

This was a huge opportunity. The only catch was that it wasn't a paid gig . . . at first. I would enter a one-year apprenticeship and would be responsible for raising my own monthly financial support. However, from my initial correspondence with ECM, I learned there was a probable chance to be hired upon completion of my 12-month commitment. The challenge would be raising enough financial support to pay for the apprenticeship *and* my car payments, insurance, and other miscellaneous expenses.

I prayed. I fasted. I pleaded with God for confirmation and direction. But even before I prayed, I knew in my heart that I was supposed to go. Still, I didn't want to make an emotional decision, so I waited for God's confirmation. It came on three separate occasions by way of three individuals.

The first confirmation occurred at a youth conference I attended in Ohio. During the post-message worship and altar-ministry time, the speaker—who was from California and whom I had never seen before in my life—approached me and said, "I feel strongly that God wants me to tell you that he is getting ready to move you to another state, and he is going to open doors you never dreamed would be possible, so don't be afraid to go."

This out-of-the-blue confirmation brought me to tears and gave me Holy Ghost goosebumps. Done. I was in— hook, line, and sinker. I didn't need another confirmation, but God gave me two more anyway.

The second confirmation came during a trip to Phoenix to visit my ailing grandmother. While in town, I drove over to Phoenix First Assembly of God to meet with Brad Baker, who was the youth pastor at the time. After a brief visit, I spent some time in prayer on the church's Prayer Mountain. By the time I flew home to Ohio, I had a settled peace that I was making the right decision.

The third confirmation came after driving to Tulsa to visit ECM's ministry headquarters and meet the staff. I had hoped to meet with Eastman Curtis in person, but he was out of town. Still, he took the time to call me, and I was grateful for that. Before leaving Tulsa, I went to the Oral Roberts University Prayer Tower to cry out to God one last time before making my final decision. (By the way, I don't believe you need a prayer tower or three confirmations to hear from God—but God used all of the above in my journey.)

Not long after my final return to Ohio, I threw all of my belongings into a U-Haul and headed to the Bible Belt, where sweet tea, big hair, and live music reigned; megachurches were on every corner; high school football was worshiped; and tornadoes were the real deal. Tulsa is the only town I've ever lived in where you can drive past a fender bender only to find the two drivers holding hands in prayer instead of fighting.

I spent almost four years in Tulsa before moving back home to Illinois to plant the church that I still pastor today. Just three months into my apprenticeship at ECM, our director moved to Florida to pastor a church, and I was thrust into his role. By the end of my first year, I was on paid staff, developing the new internship program, managing our regional youth conventions, and ghostwriting for Eastman. During my second year there, Annette and I got married, and she was hired by ECM not long after. In Tulsa I was able to travel, preach, write, act (as a television and movie extra), work in radio, coproduce a national television show, and even do some stand-up comedy. While in Oklahoma, we attended Church on the Move on Sunday mornings and Guts Church on Sunday nights (which is where I got the vision to plant RockChurch).

But everything I just mentioned almost didn't happen.

Why? Because I almost didn't go to Tulsa. I almost missed out on some of the greatest opportunities, relationships, and experiences of my life—not to mention some bona fide training ground for future ministry—all because I didn't want to disappoint some people.

Once I had made up my mind to go and had announced it to my pastor and the church, I began to encounter a lot of "you're making a mistake" talk. Several parents of teenagers in my youth group questioned my decision. I understood why (to an extent), but ultimately they were coming to conclusions based on what was best for them and their kids, though they would probably have said the opposite.

It was also going to be hard to leave my pastor. In fact, that was the hardest part of the decision because he wasn't just my pastor; he also had been my youth pastor when I was in high school. He had been instrumental in helping me navigate which Bible college to attend, and while I was in college he and I had talked about my being his youth pastor when he became a senior pastor. Everything had gone as planned, but now, after two years, I was leaving.

I was torn, and so was he. Although he was excited for my opportunity, it was difficult for him not to take it personally. We were like family. I practically lived with him. Now that I'm a senior pastor myself, I understand why he was upset; but at the time I took it personally. I absolutely did not want to upset or disappoint him, but I believed I was making the right decision. To make matters even more difficult, my parents also felt I was making a mistake—at least at the beginning. That was brutal.

Have you ever intentionally made the wrong decision because it was easier or because you wanted to avoid conflict? That's where I was. I didn't want to be the bad guy. I didn't want anyone mad at me. I didn't like that people I loved and cared about believed I was making a mistake. I allowed doubt to creep in, and I almost teetered the wrong way. But in the end, I knew that my highest accountability was to God. "We must obey God rather than any human authority."[5]

If God tells you to do something, you'd better do it, no matter what anyone else says.

This is another reason why it's so important to know God's voice. Please don't misunderstand me. I'm not saying you shouldn't listen to wise counsel or that you should blow off the advice of a multitude of counselors. But I am saying that if God tells you to do something, you'd better do it, no matter what anyone else says. Of course, you had better be 100 percent certain that it's God who is speaking and not the anchovy pizza you ate at midnight. The best way to discern whether something comes from God is to weigh it against Scripture.

SHAKE IT OFF AND SHOUT LOUDER

One of my favorite stories in the New Testament is about a blind man named Bartimaeus. Mark's Gospel sets the scene by saying that Jesus and his disciples were leaving the city of Jericho with a large crowd following them. These people weren't following Jesus out of fear that they would otherwise go to hell. They had much more immediate and compelling reasons. The crowds followed Jesus because he had compassion for them, healed them, fed them, and spent time with them. It's easy to follow Jesus when you know he's *for* you. If anyone ever tells you that Jesus doesn't love you—shake it off!

I'm sure Bartimaeus had heard that Jesus was unstopping deaf ears, popping open blind eyes, and causing the crippled and lame to walk and leap for joy. Moreover, demon-possessed folks were being set free, and thousands of people had been fed with a little boy's sack lunch. Not only that, but apparently this Jesus dude could walk on water, calm a storm, and raise a little girl from the dead. One woman had fought through a crowd and received her healing just by touching Jesus' robe. So yeah, Jesus was a rock star, and everyone—including Bartimaeus—wanted to be around him.

Bartimaeus was not only blind; he was a beggar who survived by sitting at the roadside and asking people for a handout. How humiliating that must have been! Yet it was all he knew.

Bartimaeus heard that Jesus was passing by. This was his chance, his one shot at a better life. Imagine his excitement! I bet that all he could think about was how amazing it would be to have his sight. Although he couldn't see, he had vision, and he was about to embrace it.

Jesus is going to walk right past me! Come on, Bart, make it happen! Listen for his voice and tackle him if you have to!

The Scripture says that when Bartimaeus heard that Jesus was nearby, he began to shout, "Jesus, Son of David, have mercy on me!"[6]

Yes! You did it! Woot! Slam dunk, Bart! Boom shakalaka!

Not so fast. "Be quiet!" the bystanders yelled at him.

No! This isn't supposed to happen. It can't end like this.

If this has ever happened to you, you know there's nothing worse than being excited about something—an idea, vision, dream, potential miracle, breakthrough, second chance, new chapter, opportunity, healing, or restoration—only to have somebody shoot you down.

Shake it off.

"Hope deferred makes the heart sick, but a dream fulfilled is a tree of life."[7] I'm sure Bartimaeus was sick to his stomach at that moment. I've been there.

Shake it off.

Hey guys, I'm moving to Tulsa to work for a national youth ministry.

"You're making a mistake."

Shake it off.

I'm leaving Oklahoma to plant a rock 'n' roll church in Illinois for the unchurched and dechurched.

"What a stupid idea to leave job security."

Shake it off.

Bartimaeus wasn't about to let the haters and naysayers crush his dream. It was either dismiss the doubters or remain a blind beggar for the rest of his life. So what did he do? He shook it off and dismissed the doubters by crying out to Jesus even louder. I can picture him screaming as loud as he could, with all his might—fighting for life or death, sight or blindness, miracle or disappointment, victory or defeat. He could either succumb to their discouragement and intimidation or smash fear in the mouth.

Jesus, Son of David, have mercy on me!

Jesus stopped. Bartimaeus had gotten his attention. "Tell him to come here," Jesus said.

What happened next is remarkable. The people called Bartimaeus and said, "Cheer up. Come on, he's calling you!"[8] Just like that they went from telling him to shut up to prodding him toward Jesus.

"Hey, Bartimaeus! Shut up! Jesus doesn't have time for you! . . . Wait, what, Jesus? Bring him to you? Oh. Okay. Hey, Bartimaeus! Wait! Our bad. Come here! Jesus wants to talk to you."

Shake it off.

This is my favorite part of the story. Jesus asks a question that will change Bartimaeus's life forever. And it's the same question he's asking you and me: "What do you want me to do for you?"

Bartimaeus answers, "I want to see!"[9]

Bam! Done!

Sight. Colors. Shapes. Grass. Trees. Dirt. People. Smiles.

Nine words from Jesus and one answer from Bartimaeus kick off the first day of the rest of his life. Had Bartimaeus not shaken off the doubters, he would have died a blind beggar.

Bartimaeus shook off words of doubt.

David shook off words of doubt.

I had to shake off words of doubt.

What about you?

Have you allowed the words of those around you—whether friend or foe—to keep you from hearing Jesus?

What do you want me to do for you?

Have you allowed words of doubt to stop you from embracing your cause? Have you allowed yourself to be knocked down by negativity?

Shake it off.

SHAKING OFF NEGATIVE THOUGHTS

It hurts to have those whom you love and trust shoot down your dreams. And while it's tough to deal with doubters, it's even more difficult when the doubter is *you*. If you kick around negative thoughts long enough, you will start to believe them. And if you start to believe them, you will begin to second-guess yourself and even question God.

I'm not qualified.

I don't think I can do this.

It's probably never going to happen for me.

Did God really say what I think he said?

> **Have you allowed the words of those around you—whether friend or foe—to keep you from hearing Jesus?**

So what should we do to combat these kinds of thoughts? To borrow a phrase: "Tell the negative committee that meets in your head to sit down and shut up." The best way to do that is to invest yourself in the Word of God. "Fix your thoughts on what is true, and honorable, and right, and pure, and lovely, and admirable. Think about things that are excellent and worthy of praise."[10]

When God says that he has good plans for us and good works for us to walk in, we have to believe him.[11] Sure, bad things sometimes happen to good people. Things don't always work out the way we want them to. But we still have to trust God.

We must dismiss the doubt and allow our faith to increase so we can slay our giants.

Personally, when I'm struggling, I love to read the book of Psalms.

"I praise you, for I am fearfully and wonderfully made."[12]

"For you bless the godly, O LORD; you surround them with your shield of love."[13]

"GOD puts the fallen on their feet again and pushes the wicked into the ditch."[14]

"GOD charts the road you take."[15]

"[God] counts the stars and assigns each a name. Our Lord is great, with limitless strength; we'll never comprehend what he knows and does."[16]

God is our refuge and strength, always ready to help in times of trouble.[17]

It's important to shake off negative thoughts and dismiss your doubts because you don't want to become a negative person. Negativity starts in your head, moves to your heart, and comes out of your mouth. "Out of the abundance of the heart the mouth speaks."[18] If you guard your heart and your mind, you won't have to muzzle your mouth. The last thing you want to do is morph into Debbie Downer or Mr. Negativity.

We need to see ourselves the way God sees us—as victors and overcomers. "Everyone who has been born of God overcomes the world. And this is the victory that has overcome the world—our faith."[19] That's a lesson that Gideon had to learn.

God saw Gideon as a mighty man of valor. Gideon saw himself as a failure. In fact, when God sent an angel to commission him to save Israel from the oppression of the Midianites, Gideon was hiding. The angel said, "You're a mighty man of valor, a mighty hero, and a mighty warrior. The Lord is with you."[20] Gideon responded, "Uh, you got the wrong guy. My family is weak, and I'm the weakest of the weak."[21] Gideon's self-doubt and negativity were on full display, but God wasn't deterred by that.

"Gideon," the Lord answered, "you can rescue Israel because I am going to help you! Defeating the Midianites will be as easy as beating up one man."[22]

Well, if you put it that way . . .

I recently saw a tweet that said, "Water can't sink a ship unless it gets inside." So even if you're surrounded by negativity, it can't take you down unless you allow it to get inside. Shake it off.

I had to battle doubt and discouragement when my mom was in the hospital fighting a pericardial infection for almost seven weeks in 2009. I pretty much lived at the hospital during this time and for the first few weeks after she was moved to intensive care. This meant countless hours in the ICU family waiting room. To say it was depressing is like saying you get wet when you swim. Everyone in an ICU waiting room is sad. Most are receiving bad news, and it's hard to stay positive when you're surrounded by grief. I was so burdened by the cumulative weight of my own concerns for my mom and everyone else's grief for their loved ones that I finally decided to move my little office from the ICU waiting room to the cafeteria. Where there's food, there's happiness, right? People laugh in the cafeteria. People eat, hang out, visit, and get a break from the mental fog. I can honestly say that the change in atmosphere helped me make it through that time.

Even if you're surrounded by negativity, it can't take you down unless you allow it to get inside. Shake it off.

DON'T DELIVER DOUBT

I don't know who created it, but I saw a picture of a birthday cake recently with the following meme: *Blowing out someone else's candles doesn't make yours shine any brighter.*

Don't be a candle-blower-outer! (That's not even a real word, but don't be one.) The world doesn't need any more pessimism. If you're a Negative Nelly, Debbie Downer, or

Bobby Buzzkill, we all still love you, but please allow me to politely encourage you to *knock it off*!

Don't deliver doubt. It's hard enough to shake off the words of doubt that are rattling around in our own brains, so let's not add to the problem. Let's make it a point not to be one of those people who always brings discouragement. I know they prefer to call it *realism*, but if you're the one who is always derailing somebody else's dream . . . well, it's just not cool.

We all know at least one person who seemingly cannot be happy about anything.

You say, "Wasn't that a great service?"

They say, "No, I didn't like the color of the pastor's shirt."

What? Don't be that person!

Who cares about the color of the pastor's shirt? Be happy! Besides, he picked that shirt out himself and it's one of his favorites.

If you're on Facebook, or if you read the comments on just about any article you can find online, you see the rising tide of negativity every day. Let me say this as gently as I can: If the majority of your online or social-media posts are rants, you're part of the problem.

I'm not saying that you should never vent. We all vent. There are times when we all get frustrated. But there are some people who post something negative every single day!

It's too hot.

It's too cold.

I don't like the president—or the people running for president.

All Christians are hypocrites.

I don't like my job.

If you shop at _____, you're supporting the devil.

Here are eight reasons why you're going to hell.

If you don't type AMEN or share this post, you don't really love Jesus.

Don't send your kids to that school. They hate kids.

Don't give your business to _____. Their bathrooms are disgusting.

I love my church, but _____.

If we change the way we *think*, we will change the way we *talk*. If we change the way we *talk*, we will change the way we *act*.

Should I keep going? No! It's too familiar, isn't it? And here's the catch: If we start listening to them, we'll start acting like them. Let's be part of the solution instead. If we change the way we *think*, we will change the way we *talk*. If we change the way we *talk*, we will change the way we *act*. Let's think, talk, and act positively.

THAT'S NOT THE HALF OF IT

If there's anyone in Scripture who understands the phrase "shake it off," it would be Paul. Check out what he went through:

> I've worked much harder, been jailed more often, beaten up more times than I can count, and at death's door time after time. I've been flogged five times with the Jews' thirty-nine lashes, beaten by Roman rods three times, pummeled with rocks once. I've been shipwrecked three times, and immersed in

the open sea for a night and a day. In hard traveling year in and year out, I've had to ford rivers, fend off robbers, struggle with friends, struggle with foes. I've been at risk in the city, at risk in the country, endangered by desert sun and sea storm, and betrayed by those I thought were my brothers. I've known drudgery and hard labor, many a long and lonely night without sleep, many a missed meal, blasted by the cold, naked to the weather.[23]

Jailed more often. Paul was in prison multiple times. He even wrote part of the New Testament from behind bars. That's called prison ministry from the inside.

Beaten up more times than I can count. I was 0–1 as a young fighter. But if I had gotten beaten up several times, I probably would have stayed away from people or hired Ronda Rousey to be my bodyguard.

At death's door time after time. Can you say *bulletproof*?

Flogged five times with thirty-nine lashes. Paul would have had the scars to prove it. A lot of people died during that kind of severe beating. Paul endured such a beating on five occasions.

Beaten by Roman rods three times. I haven't researched what a Roman rod is, but I can tell you that I've cried after getting hit with a Wiffle ball bat.

Pummeled with rocks. And I thought paintball was bad!

Shipwrecked three times. After the first time, you couldn't pay me to get back on a boat. After the second time, you couldn't pay me to go to the beach. After three times, you couldn't pay me to take a bath. And if after one of those shipwrecks, I swam to shore, built a campfire to keep warm, and got bitten by a viper? Well, that would just about do me in. But not Paul, apparently. When he got bitten by a viper, he simply shook it off into the fire.[24] Can we agree right now that Paul is the man? I can just imagine what he would have tweeted: *So here was my day: Shipwrecked. Treaded water. Swam to shore. Built fire with bare hands. Got bitten by viper. Shook it off. #RoutineDay.*

Immersed in the open sea for a night and a day. While on a missions trip to Jamaica when I was 16, we had a day off to go snorkeling in the Caribbean via sailboat. Our sailboat captain's name was Hector the Protector.

Shipwrecked. Treaded water. Swam to shore. Built fire with bare hands. Got bitten by viper. Shook it off. #RoutineDay.

Seriously?

"Yeah, mon!"

After our snorkeling excursion, Hector the Protector anchored the sailboat a couple hundred yards from the shore to wait for the little motorboats to pick us up and ferry us to the dock. He asked whether anyone on our team dared to swim back instead of waiting for the boats.

I thought, *No problem, mon!* I dove off the sailboat and began my swim. (I was 16 and stupid—what can I say?)

About halfway to the dock, my mind reminded me that I had watched *Jaws* a week before our trip. I also remembered that I had cut my knee earlier in the day while snorkeling.

Blood. Sharks. *Swim faster!*

I had a full-blown panic attack that would have resulted in a world record had someone been timing me. I looked like a bathtub toy powered by a car battery. That frantic freestyle swim in the ocean lasted only about 10 or 15 minutes, but it *felt* like a night and a day.

Struggle with friends, struggle with foes. Have you ever been betrayed by someone you love? That's rough. That hurts worse than being pummeled with a pile of rocks.

After finishing his spiel, Paul adds, in his best TV-infomercial voice: *But wait, there's more![25]*

> And that's not the half of it, when you throw in
> the daily pressures and anxieties of all the churches.
> When someone gets to the end of his rope, I feel the
> desperation in my bones. When someone is duped
> into sin, an angry fire burns in my gut.[26]

As a pastor, I understand Paul's remark about "the daily pressures and anxieties of all the churches." I'm responsible for just one church, yet I have experienced a plethora of problems: stress, anxiety, drama, setbacks, hurts, transitions, and heartaches. Paul planted several churches, and he had those daily pressures and anxieties in spades.

Ministry is tough. Pastoring can be rough. It is also the most rewarding job and greatest blessing I have ever experienced. Most of the people I've met along the way have been awesome.

One last thing. Paul is also the guy who wrote from jail, "Rejoice in the Lord always."[27]

That last word just kills me.

Always.

Not some of the time.
Always.
Not most of the time.
Always.
Always?
Always.

In the storm. In the open sea. After you swim to shore. After you are bitten by a viper. After you are pummeled with rocks. After you are punched in the face. After someone lies about you. After you go to jail for doing the right thing. After you fail. After you file for bankruptcy. After you lose your job. After you lose a loved one. After your marriage falls apart. After you get demoted. After your car gets repossessed. After you have a miscarriage. After you get bullied. After you flunk out of school. After your house burns down. After your property is foreclosed on. After your electricity gets shut off. After your water gets shut off. After your debit card won't work at the grocery store. After your best friend betrays you. After the school calls you to pick up your rebellious child. After you find out that you have cancer. After your new business fails. After the judge finds you guilty. After your church plant falls short of expectations. After someone else gets the promotion.

And that's not the half of it.

#41WillCome
#ShakeItOff
#Rejoice

RAWK STANCE

*I have done this to both lions and bears, and I'll do it to this pagan
Philistine, too, for he has defied the armies of the living God!*

1 SAMUEL 17:36, NLT

Failure to prepare is preparing to fail.

JOHN WOODEN

"Now you played hard in here, people, and I am proud
of every last stinking one of you. So let's just give this everything we got. We may fall on our faces, but if we do, we will
fall with dignity! With a guitar in our hands and rock in our
hearts! And in the words of AC/DC: 'We roll tonight to the
guitar bite . . . and for those about to rock . . . I salute you.'"

Jack Black's stouthearted speech in the movie *School of
Rock* is meant to motivate and fire up his students as they
prepare to take the stage in the Battle of the Bands. If you
have seen the movie or have attended a rock concert or two,
then you're familiar with the rawk stance! This is the pose
where a musician spreads his legs, clutches his guitar with
one hand and lifts up his other fist in a heavy-metal salute.
In fact, I just grabbed an air guitar and jumped into my

imaginary rawk stance . . . in the East Peoria Public Library, where I'm writing.

No, I'm not kidding.

And for a wannabe musician like me—I'll be honest; it felt pretty good.

When rock stars get into their rawk stance, what they are really doing is getting into position. Their posture screams, "I'm ready to rock!" They are prepared for whatever comes next. Their prior blood, sweat, and tears—from each intense practice, rehearsal, and walk-through—finally come to fruition.

Practice produces results. Preparation precedes payoff. Hustle helps people win. If we want to hold on and stand strong until our 41 comes, the fifth key is to *prepare in order to receive a payoff.*

Keys to help you hold on when life gets tough and stand strong until a new day dawns

1. Know your enemy.
2. Embrace your cause.
3. Smash fear in the mouth.
4. Shake off doubts and doubters.
5. Prepare in order to receive a payoff.

PRACTICE MATTERS

Like a lot of people who thrive on caffeine, I spend a lot of time at the local Starbucks. My drink of choice is a venti caramel white-chocolate iced mocha with an extra shot of espresso, nonfat, no whip. Depending on which barista is working, I may not even have to say my order. They know. In fact, a couple of years ago, my wife pulled up to the drive-through window in my car and the barista smiled and said, "So . . . you're the wife." So yeah, I'm there a lot.

Long before the "red cup controversy" blew up into a national news story, Starbucks would occasionally print inspirational quotes on their cups. Check out what Rev Run from the supergroup Run-DMC said about practice. It was printed on the side of a Starbucks cup as *The Way I See It #93*. These are great words about the importance of practice.

> The one reason that my group Run-DMC was on point was practice! My motto is: If I miss a day of practice, I know it. If I miss two days of practice, my manager knows it. If I miss three days, my audience knows it! Practice, practice, practice!

Apparently, former Philadelphia 76ers basketball star Allen Iverson didn't get Rev Run's memo. Though Iverson played fourteen years in the NBA and won Rookie of the Year, league MVP, and All-Star Game MVP awards during his storied career, he is perhaps best known among the YouTube crowd for an epic interview meltdown after reporters called into question his work ethic because he had missed a practice.

> If I can't practice, I can't practice, man. If I'm hurt, I'm hurt. I mean, simple as that. . . . I mean, listen, we're talking about practice. Not a game. Not a game. Not a game . . . not the game that I go out

there and die for, and play every game like it's my last; not the game. We're talking about *practice*, man. I mean, how *silly* is that? We're talking about practice. . . . We ain't talking about the game. We're talking about practice, man. When you come to the arena, and you see me play, you see me play, don't you? You see me give everything I got, right? But we're talking about *practice* right now.[1]

Let's talk about practice, shall we? I had someone tell me a long time ago that "practice does not make perfect. Only perfect practice makes perfect."

Are you engaged? Are you giving 110 percent?

Uh, no. No one can give 110 percent, Chuck.

Okay, but we can give 100 percent. We can give it our all. To practice is to commit. Are you committed to prepare yourself for what lies ahead?

If we're not willing to prepare ourselves to slay our giants, accomplish our visions, or fulfill our destinies; if we're not willing to pursue our goals, then we're far less likely to accomplish them. Period.

Based on Allen Iverson's rant, we can assume that he was all about the *game*. The game, the game, the game—not practice, not practice, not practice. But even Iverson didn't just show up in the gym one day as an awesome player. He practiced plenty to get there. A lot of people don't like practice, but winners know how valuable it is. Practice is painful, but it prepares us for the game.

When David's sanity was called into question after he

announced to King Saul that he would fight Goliath, here's how he responded:

> "I have been taking care of my father's sheep and goats," he said. "When a lion or a bear comes to steal a lamb from the flock, I go after it with a club and rescue the lamb from its mouth. If the animal turns on me, I catch it by the jaw and club it to death. I have done this to both lions and bears, and I'll do it to this pagan Philistine, too, for he has defied the armies of the living God!"[2]

Allow me to say out loud what you are probably already thinking: *David is the man!* How can you not be a fan of a kid who can grab a lion by the jaw and club it to death? Are you kidding me?

We're not talking about a mere dog here—David goes *beast mode* on a lion! For the record, if I ever happen to be attacked by a lion after risking my life to take a selfie, I will either (1) shoot the lion with the gun I don't have; (2) hit it with my car (though I guess he can't attack me if I'm in my car); or (3) run away as fast as I can while making exaggerated promises to God. Yep, I'm toast.

I love how David throws it out there like it's no big deal. *So, Dave, what did you do today?*

"You know, not much. Took the sheep to the watering hole, grabbed my harp and wrote a new ballad, skipped a few rocks across a stream, destroyed a lion with my bare hands. Just a typical day out in the field."

All joking aside, David had already positioned himself for his fight with Goliath because of his past encounters with a lion and a bear. He had practiced! He was also skilled with a slingshot—no doubt through hours of practice—but ultimately, it was God who prepared David for battle.

What does this mean for you and me? Every place we go is preparation for where God is taking us. God can use our past experiences—good and bad—to prepare us for future battles. We must be willing to work and learn.

> **Every place we go is preparation for where God is taking us. God can use our past experiences—good and bad—to prepare us for future battles.**

In his book *The 21 Most Powerful Minutes in a Leader's Day*, John Maxwell writes,

> Everyone loves an opportunity. But many people want an opportunity to come to them before they start improving themselves to capitalize on it. They think, *When I get the position, then I'll start growing.* That's doing things backward. David had it right. He grew first, lifting his personal lids, and by the time his big opportunity came, he was ready for it.[3]

HUSTLE HELPS YOU WIN

A few weeks ago, I saw an Instagram post that was a photograph of a sign that read, *Dreams only work if you do.* In other words, hustle helps you win. Remember, failing to prepare is preparing to fail.

If you're not taking steps to prepare yourself, your vision

will remain a distant dream. It's not enough to have a vision. It's not even enough to write it down. You must be willing to pick it up and run with it. You must be eager to *work*. The vision for this book began a long time ago—I'm talking more than a decade. But for years it remained dormant, because all I did was talk about it. It took a lot of work, a lot of hustle, and a lot of Starbucks to finally knock it out!

Vision requires preparation, hustle, and discipline.

Preparation requires hustle and discipline.

Hustle requires discipline.

Notice that *discipline* is the common denominator. Paul writes: "All athletes are disciplined in their training. They do it to win a prize that will fade away, but we do it for an eternal prize."[4] Successful athletes discipline themselves. Yes, I'm talking about practice, but no one said it would be easy. "No discipline is enjoyable while it is happening—it's painful! But afterward there will be a peaceful harvest of right living for those who are trained in this way."[5] Most people don't like training at first. But the payoff in the end makes it worth it.

I used to hate running—unless I was running to the fridge. It took discipline to start using my "Couch to 5K" running app. It was excruciating torture . . . in the beginning. Now I love to run. I've gone from hating it to actually craving it. I look forward to putting on my headphones and taking off for my nightly two-mile run. I dream while I run. I pray while I run. I plan while I run. I remember things when I run. I get new ideas when I run. It's almost as if I forget that I'm actually doing work. And now I'm much healthier because of it.

I love sports and especially enjoy watching the NFL,

NBA, and MLB play-offs. There's nothing more exciting in sports than the end of the season—whether it's the Super Bowl, the NBA championship, or the World Series. Why? Because we get to see all the individual and team hustle and preparation pay off when the champions are crowned.

What happens when they win? Everyone storms the field for some good old-fashioned celebratory mayhem: Gatorade baths, champagne showers, and trophy hoisting. And it all happens because coaches and players were willing to train, practice, prepare, and hustle while running with a vision that was laid out at the beginning of the season. Ask a trophy-clutching winner drenched in sweat and Gatorade whether it was worth it. Ask Kelly Clarkson or Carrie Underwood whether their preparation and hustle before they won *American Idol* was worth it.

START TODAY

What is the key to preparation? Start today. The journey of a thousand miles begins with a single step.[6]

One of the most fascinating stories of preparation in the Bible is found in the book of Exodus. Moses and Pharaoh were in the middle of a showdown over the freedom of the Israelites. God had called Moses, through a burning bush in the desert, to rescue the Israelites from Egypt. The only obstacle standing in the way was Mr. Stubborn himself—Pharaoh. Here is a quick summary of how things progressed after the first plague:

Moses: "Let my people go!"

Pharaoh: "No!"

Moses: "Then deal with this plague."

Pharaoh: "My bad. You can go."

Moses: "Okay, the plague is gone."

Pharaoh: "Wait, I changed my mind."

The second plague consisted of God sending a swarm of frogs from the Nile River. Frogs were everywhere! They were in every home. They were in every room. They were in every bed. They were in every oven. They were in every bowl. They were on every person.

My son, Ashton, has a frog named Zipper. Zipper peed on me last week while Ashton was holding him. In fact, he has peed every single time someone has held him during the three weeks we've had him. One frog is enough. I cannot imagine having frogs everywhere in our house. I certainly cannot imagine having them swarming our city.

Egypt was infested with frogs! I have no doubt that it was so bad that a nasty stench permeated the entire nation. Pharaoh summoned Moses to find relief, but when Moses asked, "When do you want me to make it stop? When do you want me to get rid of the frogs?" Pharaoh gave an answer that must have puzzled Moses and still has people scratching their heads today.

"Tomorrow."[7]

Not "right now."

Not "immediately."

Not "five minutes ago."

Tomorrow.

How arrogant is that? How prideful? How callous do you have to be to make your people live in that mess for another day? The plague could have been stopped in an instant. But no.

Whatever plague you're facing, whatever giant, what are you doing about it? You have a vision. You know your cause. Are you running with it? Go! Start now.

SEIZE YOUR MOMENT

Thomas Edison said, "Good fortune often happens when opportunity meets with preparation."[8] If you will take the time and effort *today* to prepare, work, and hustle, when God opens your door *tomorrow*, you will be ready to seize the moment.

When I was in my early twenties and working for ECM in Tulsa, I received a call from Eastman Curtis one morning while I was leading devotions for about 20 interns.

"Hey, Chuck! I'm supposed to preach at Victory Christian Center's high school today, and I need you to do it."

"Uh."

> **If you will take the time and effort *today* to prepare, work, and hustle, when God opens your door *tomorrow*, you will be ready to seize the moment.**

"Do you have a message burning in your heart?" he added excitedly.

Before I tell you what my answer was, let me first inform you that Victory Christian Center at the time was one of the largest churches in Tulsa—several thousand people. Not only that, but the senior pastor was Billy Joe Daugherty (now deceased), who was very well known and respected world-wide in charismatic circles.

There were about 500 high school students and they were all expecting to hear from one of the most sought-after youth evangelists in the 1990s—Eastman Curtis. Nobody knew who Chuck Tate was. My answer was a no-brainer.

"I don't think I can do it," I said nervously.

"Come on, man! Don't you have a sugar stick you can pull out?"

"No . . . I'm not ready. I'm not prepared."

But Eastman was not that easily dissuaded.

"Come on, Chuck! You can do it! You can do it! I know you've got something burning in your heart that you can share with those kids."

Well, I couldn't say no to that. The truth was that I was honored to be asked, but I was freaked out because I wasn't prepared. But I caved anyway.

"Okay. I'll do it," I said. "How much time do I have?"

"Twenty minutes."

"It's going to take me twenty minutes to get there," I pleaded.

"Then you better get going."

Click.

On the way to Victory Christian Center, I glanced down at what I was wearing.

Why am I wearing white painter pants today?

Seriously, that day is the only time in my life that I can recall wearing painter pants.

These kids are going to take one look at me and say, "Who is this idiot you have sent to us?"

So, yeah, I was oozing with confidence.

When I arrived at the school, I thought, *Well, at least Billy Joe won't be here.*

Wrong. When I walked into the lobby, there he was, waiting for me. He took one look at me, and I could tell he was concerned. Did I mention I was rocking a mullet? He was clearly nervous, and that made me even more nervous. I knew he was thinking, *Oh great! Eastman failed to mention he was sending Billy Ray Cyrus!*

My confidence was pretty much shot at that point.

Literally five minutes after I met Pastor Billy Joe, I was onstage being introduced to hundreds of high school kids.

Well, at least maybe Billy Joe will leave now.

Wrong again. Pastor Billy Joe walked up the aisle, sat down in the front row, folded his arms, and looked at me as if to say, *Okay, Mullet Boy! Let's see what you got.*

I preached a message that day that I had done only one or two other times. It was called "41 Will Come."

I wish I could tell you that I blew everyone away and the message ushered in a revival that lasted for the rest of the school year. But that didn't happen. It wasn't horrible; it wasn't great. But I made it through, the kids responded, and Pastor Billy Joe even wrote me a letter of recommendation afterward.

But guess what? I felt I had missed an opportunity because I was unprepared. I learned something from that experience, and I promised myself that the next time I got a phone call like that, I would be prepared to preach.

That phone call came just a few years later.

Not too long after we planted our church in Illinois, Annette and I returned to Tulsa for a visit. As we were pulling into town, Angel Curtis called and said, "Hey, Chuck! Eastman needs you to help him out tomorrow with something. Are you in?"

"Absolutely," I said. "We're just excited to see you guys. What does he need?"

Angel said that Eastman wanted me to host the regional television program *Praise the Lord* on the Trinity Broadcasting Network.

"What?" I said. "Are you messing with me? I don't think I'm ready for that. I can't do that."

So on my way to do the show the next morning (yeah, I know, I can be talked into anything), I received a phone call from the station, during which I was politely informed that the program was not a 60-minute taped show as I had thought. It was a 90-minute *live* broadcast!

What have I gotten myself into?

Upon my arrival at the studio, I was introduced to the producer. She took one look at me and seemed more concerned than Billy Joe Daugherty had been when I showed up to do chapel. My mullet was gone, but I was still an unknown minister who was about to host a popular television program in place of Eastman Curtis (who by that time was pastoring one of the fastest-growing churches in America).

I was given the following detailed instructions:

- There will be three cameras. Look in the direction of whichever camera is lit up.
- Keep your eye on the producer, who will hold up cue cards in place of a teleprompter.
- You will interview two musical artists. You will be given predetermined questions printed on index cards.

The interview part freaked me out and affected my confidence because I'm hearing impaired but had not yet purchased hearing aids. The only breaks I would get during the broadcast would be when they cut away to show a music video for each of the two artists I was interviewing. After both interviews were completed, I would take time to pray for all the prayer requests that were called in during the show up to that point. The final segment of the program would consist of my preaching for however much time remained.

Uh, I could have used that information last night. No notes, no problem. Right, Chuck?

I have a lot of respect for anyone who's involved in live television. My first interview, with the lead singer of a rock band, was rough to say the least. Great guy. Great band. Horrible interview. He answered every question with about one word. My hearing wasn't an issue because *yes* and *no* are pretty easy words to hear.

Sheesh, dude! Help me out! No more one-word responses. Please!

After rifling through the predetermined questions in about two minutes, I began asking whatever I could think of.

What's your favorite color?

What's your shoe size?

What's your favorite cereal?

Okay, not really, but we went through the preset material so fast that the producer began writing down questions on a dry-erase board for me to ask. One of those questions was, *Ask him to share his testimony.*

"So, why don't you share your testimony with us."

"Well, I gave my life to Christ and started a band."

Somebody just shoot me!

The second interview was fantastic because it was with a hip-hop artist who got to preaching. I was like, *I love you, man! Can I just stop and give you a hug right now?*

The only really awkward moment came when I looked into the camera (yes, the one that was lit up) and announced that I was going to begin praying for all the prayer requests that had been called in. Out of the corner of my eye, I saw the producer frantically shaking her head from left to right. I glanced at the whiteboard, but there were no instructions there. Did I mention we were *live?*

I had no idea what to do next, so I ignored the head shaking, bowed my own head, and started praying. When I finished, I realized I was going to have to preach for roughly 20 minutes. But guess what? This time I was ready. Having learned a valuable lesson from my previous near-disaster, I was ready to preach impromptu.

Great feedback.

Great response.

New confidence.

Why? I came prepared. (#SeizeYourMoment)

VISION WITHOUT SIGHT

During the 1956 Rose Bowl, a once-in-a-lifetime opportunity presented itself for second-string kicker Dave Kaiser of Michigan State. The Spartans were playing the defending national champion UCLA Bruins, and the score was deadlocked at 14–14. Dave's role that year had been limited to kickoffs and long-distance kicks, and his number wasn't called until the game was on the line.

Most kickers line up from the side, but Dave Kaiser was a straight-ahead kicker, so he lined up directly behind the ball.

Snap.

Kick.

After kicking the ball, instead of watching the ball sail through the sky, Dave turned to look at the referee . . . and waited for the signal.

Talk about pressure. Field-goal kickers are either heroes or goats. It's either seize the moment or seize up and blow it. That had to have been the longest three seconds of Dave's life. If he made it, he would walk off the field a hero. If he missed, he would be dismissed by many as a loser and most likely would go home alone.

When the ball sailed through the uprights and the referee threw his hands in the air, it confirmed that Dave Kaiser would leave the stadium a hero.

After the game, Duffy Daugherty, Michigan State's head

coach, asked Dave why he had watched the referee instead of the ball.

"Coach, I left my contact lenses in the locker room, so I didn't know if I'd made it or not. I couldn't see the goalposts, so I had to watch the referee."

He couldn't see the goalposts, and he had little in-game experience as a kicker, but still Dave Kaiser was ready to seize his moment. He didn't need to see where the ball went. He only needed an opportunity to kick it. As it happened, it was the only field goal made by a Michigan State kicker that season.[9] But in 1999 Dave Kaiser was inducted into the Rose Bowl Hall of Fame because of it.

Helen Keller was once asked what was worse than being born blind. Her response? "Having sight without vision." Dave Kaiser was lacking his full sight during that play, but his vision was crystal clear.

By the way, that Hall of Fame Rose Bowl–winning kick just happened to be 41 yards. *Wink.* (#41WillCome)

SUIT UP

The apostle Paul tells us that we must prepare in order to stand firm against the attacks of the enemy. His exhortation is simple: Suit up.

> Put on the full armor of God, so that you can take your stand against the devil's schemes. For our struggle is not against flesh and blood, but against the rulers, against the authorities, against the powers of this dark world and against the spiritual forces

of evil in the heavenly realms. Therefore put on the full armor of God, so that *when the day of evil comes,* you may be able to stand your ground, and after you have done everything, to stand.[10]

Notice that it says "*when* the day of evil comes." It doesn't say *if;* it says *when.* We live in an evil world—a fact made increasingly obvious by all the shootings, bombings, and beheadings in recent years. And even if you don't face physical danger in that way, you still must contend with a devil who "prowls around like a roaring lion looking for someone to devour."[11] By putting on God's armor, you prepare yourself to withstand the onslaught of the enemy against you and your vision.

As you pursue God's plan to become the person he's called you to be—whether it's to launch a ministry, plant a church, start a business, build a new career, become a better parent, get through a divorce, reconcile a relationship, overcome an addiction, or whatever—it helps to know in advance that the enemy will do everything he can to sabotage you. But if you heed the words of Paul and put on your armor, you will be ready. It may not be easy, but you will be prepared to stand firm; you will be prepared to knock down every giant or obstacle that the enemy throws at you. And sometimes the entire journey is simply to prepare you for the *next* journey.

By putting on God's armor, you prepare yourself to withstand the onslaught of the enemy against you and your vision.

Paul says that after you've done everything you can to prepare, the next part is simple: *Stand.*

Do you want to stand firm when all hell breaks loose; whether you're in a downpour or in the desert; when you're wandering in the wilderness; or when you're face to face with the biggest giant of your life? Suit up.

> Put on every piece of God's armor so you will be able to resist the enemy. . . . Stand your ground, putting on the belt of truth and the body armor of God's righteousness. For shoes, put on the peace that comes from the Good News so that you will be fully prepared. In addition to all of these, hold up the shield of faith to stop the fiery arrows of the devil. Put on salvation as your helmet, and take the sword of the Spirit, which is the word of God.
> Pray in the Spirit at all times and on every occasion. Stay alert and be persistent in your prayers for all believers everywhere.[12]

Helmet of salvation?
Check.
Breastplate of righteousness?
Check.
Belt of truth?
Check.
Shoes of peace?
Check.
Shield of faith?
Check.
Sword of God's Word?

Check.

Secret weapon: prayer in the Spirit?

Check.

Now you're dressed for battle. Paul says that if you'll keep your armor on, you will still be standing when the battle is finally over.

Cue MC Hammer and holler, "Can't touch this!" (#StillStanding)

FROM PIT TO PRISON TO PALACE

One of my favorite Bible stories is the one about how God helped Joseph navigate through the ups and downs of life—including his journey from a pit to a prison cell to a palace.

Here's a recap.

Jacob had twelve sons, and Joseph was his favorite. The other sons hated Joseph because of it, so they kidnapped him and threw him into a cistern. Their jealousy almost resulted in murder, but they spared Joseph and sold him into slavery instead.

The Ishmaelite traders who purchased Joseph arrived in Egypt and pawned him off on an officer named Potiphar, the captain of Pharaoh's palace guard. God surrounded Joseph with favor and made him successful at everything he did—so much so that Potiphar took notice and made him his personal assistant.

Joseph managed Potiphar's entire household and all of his personal affairs, and God caused everything Joseph touched to flourish. Unfortunately for the young and handsome Joseph, Potiphar's wife wanted him to touch *her*. He refused.

She persisted and made sexual advances day after day. He rejected her every time and tried to stay away from her. In fact, this is what he told her: "How could I do such a wicked thing? It would be a great sin against God."[13]

One day, when no one else was around, Potiphar's wife cornered Joseph and proceeded to pounce on him. He wasn't about to let that cougar derail his destiny, so he cut loose and ran. Unfortunately, she snagged his robe and accused him of rape, so he ended up in prison—for doing the right thing.

But God was with Joseph and surrounded him with favor in prison, just as he had done when Joseph was in Potiphar's house. But that didn't mean instant freedom for Joseph. In fact, it took 13 years before he was summoned to interpret Pharaoh's dreams, and only then was he released. But he eventually ended up as the ruler of Egypt.

A few years later, Joseph was reunited with his brothers— who were now at his mercy. When their father died, they became afraid for their lives because of what they had done to Joseph as a teenager. But Joseph responded with the following words: "You intended to harm me, but God intended it all for good. He brought me to this position so I could save the lives of many people."[14]

Joseph realized that his pain in prison was part of the process. This displays remarkable character. Think about it. He didn't end up in prison for doing the wrong thing. He ended up in prison for making the right choice. It would have been easy for him to quit on God. He could have given up, but he didn't. He was confident that God was with him.

God is also with you. He can take what your enemies intend for evil and somehow produce something good— maybe even something great—if you will trust him.

This reminds me of something my friend Scot Mendenhall said recently while throwing down a stellar message at our church's Old School Meets New School revival: "When we do not trust God, we live below our potential."

> God can take what your enemies intend for evil and somehow produce something good—maybe even something great— if you will trust him.

Often, we need to trust God the most when we're in the valley, in the pit, in the prison cell, in the middle of the meantime, in the desert, in the wilderness, while facing a giant, when life is hard, when we need a second chance—that is, during times of *preparation*.

What is God preparing you for?

AMANDA'S ARMY

I hate cancer. So does my friend Amanda Noelle Wilcox.

Amanda is an extremely gifted singer and songwriter. She's an even better person. My wife and I have gotten to know her over the last few years as she has been a frequent guest of RockChurch on several occasions, performing and ministering for concerts, worship services, and a women's conference. Amanda is highly active as a worship leader in her own church—Cross Point Church in Nashville—and she has graced the stage with many noteworthy artists such as Natalie Grant, Kari Jobe, Mandisa, Plumb, Building 429,

Todd Agnew, Carlos Whittaker, and others. Both of her parents, and all four brothers and sisters, sing, so it should have come as no surprise that she practically came out of the womb singing. In fact, she remembers singing before she even learned to talk. And when I say she can sing, I mean she can *flat-out sing!*

Amanda's future in the music industry—and her future in general—took an excruciating detour on October 16, 2014, when she received news that she had stage IV colon cancer. Her boyfriend of only a few weeks at the time (now her husband) was with her when she received the crushing diagnosis. After calling her sisters and meeting with her family, Amanda took some time to process and contemplate whether she would share the news via social media. One of her good friends convinced her that, by sharing on social media, she would not only show people that she was vulnerable; she would also receive help and raise up an army of prayer warriors.

"You can do this differently than it has been done before," her friend said. "You can have joy in the midst of the storm."

A few days later, Amanda posted this message on her Facebook page:

> I was having some digestion issues, so I went in for a colonoscopy. When I woke up, the doctor, with tears in his eyes, told me he found a large tumor. Thursday they confirmed it . . . cancer. Yesterday they found spots on my liver and ovaries that they are going to test, and if they come back positive,

then I'll have Stage 4 cancer. I have to go through 5 weeks of chemo and radiation and then 8 weeks of rest before surgery to remove the tumor. I don't have health insurance, so trying to navigate paperwork and money has been a little overwhelming. But strangely enough, through this whole process I've had peace. My God is still in control. My God always had and always will take care of me. I do pray for healing, but more than that I pray that satan does not get the victory and that God would change lives through this story. "For what satan meant for evil, God meant for good." This is just the beginning of a difficult but beautiful road.

Let's start walking.

How's that for tackling one of the most challenging moments one can experience? Something powerful happens when we trust God. (#HopeForHardDays #StrengthToStand)

Amanda's new journey began, and 25,403 Facebook "likes" later, an army of supporters began walking with her and praying for her. Not only did people pray, but they began to give toward her medical expenses. Within one week of her sharing her cancer journey with the world, three fund-raising sites had been created and *Amanda's Army* T-shirts had hit the printing presses.

A few weeks later, doctors found another cancerous nodule on her thyroid. This was completely unrelated to her colon cancer. I recently asked her what was going through her mind at that exact moment.

A million things. Preparation. What does the future look like if you don't make it? What does it look like if you do? Why? Not "why me?" Just why? As in, "How did this happen?" I'm physically fit. I'm healthy. I work at a juice bar. I have no family history of cancer. I had no conclusion. It was just a strange, weird phenomenon. Still, I had decided that *God is going to take care of me no matter the outcome. God is in control no matter what.*

Notice that she said *preparation*. I'm sure that chemotherapy, radiation, and surgeries were not high on Amanda's bullet list of ways to prepare for greater things, but she gets it. *Preparation precedes payoff.* It's faith like this that pushes our tests into a testimony. It's the belief that God can use our very worst circumstances for good.

Let me make one thing clear: Cancer is not of God, and cancer is not from God. Cancer is *never* God's will. But God can take cancer (or anything else that's evil) and use it for his glory. That, my friend, is hope. That's what we cling to in times of adversity. Why? Because it's in God's Word. We either believe it or we don't. Amanda believes it.

As Amanda's journey moved forward, her army of supporters continued to walk with her. Her friend and fellow singer-songwriter Natalie Grant organized a benefit concert with performances by several well-known Christian musicians and artists. When Amanda returned home from the benefit, she posted to Instagram: "Tonight was . . . beautiful, amazing, breathtaking, encouraging and more words than I

could ever say. I feel more loved than you could ever know."
Then more chemo. More radiation. More surgeries. More challenges.

One of Amanda's surgeries was to remove her thyroid. This was a scary setback as she was faced with the possibility that her voice could be damaged beyond repair, meaning there would be a good chance she would never be able to sing again.

Still, she trusted. God answered. Surgery was successful. She would continue to sing.

Then more chemo. More radiation. More hospital visits. More getting poked like a pincushion. More steps of preparation for who knows what?

On the phone one day, I asked Amanda to tell me about her boyfriend (now husband), Reid, and how he had helped her through this journey. They had been dating for only three or four weeks when she went in for her initial colonoscopy, and it had only been six weeks when she received the diagnosis of stage IV colon cancer. So she gave him an out, an opportunity to walk away with no hard feelings.

"You didn't sign up for this," she told him. "You didn't sign up to watch me throw up and lose a lot of weight. And should our relationship progress to marriage, I have been informed that I will not be able to have kids. You have the right to leave."

He didn't walk away. Instead, he responded with the following words: "God has prepared me for this moment. I'm going to walk with you."

"He hasn't left my side," Amanda told me. "He's my rock. He's exactly what I needed."

Aren't you glad that God knows exactly what we *need*? I'm grateful that God doesn't always give us what we *want*, but he most definitely throws *what we need* our way.

I'm grateful that God doesn't always give us what we *want*, but he most definitely throws *what we need* our way.

Amanda's story is still being written, and only God knows how it will end; but at last report, the doctors consider her to be cancer-free. Regardless of what the future holds, she's walking with the very one who holds the future in his hands—and he sent an army to walk alongside her.

#41WillCome
#RawkStance
#PreparationPrecedesPayoff

BOOM GOES THE DYNAMITE!

David answered: "You've come out to fight me with a
sword and a spear and a dagger. But I've come out to
fight you in the name of the LORD All-Powerful."

1 SAMUEL 17:45, CEV

AFTER JESUS WAS BAPTIZED in the Jordan River by his cousin John, the Holy Spirit led him into the wilderness for a season of testing. The devil was waiting there, ready to administer the final exam. When Jesus had fasted for 40 days, he was hungry—who wouldn't be?—and the devil tried to take full advantage, attacking Jesus at his point of perceived weakness:

"Since you are God's Son, speak the word that will turn these stones into loaves of bread."
Jesus answered by quoting Deuteronomy: "It takes more than bread to stay alive. It takes a steady stream of words from God's mouth."

For the second test the Devil took him to the Holy City. He sat him on top of the Temple and said, "Since you are God's Son, jump." The Devil goaded him by quoting Psalm 91: "He has placed you in the care of angels. They will catch you so that you won't so much as stub your toe on a stone."

Jesus countered with another citation from Deuteronomy: "Don't you dare test the Lord your God."

For the third test, the Devil took him to the peak of a huge mountain. He gestured expansively, pointing out all the earth's kingdoms, how glorious they all were. Then he said, "They're yours—lock, stock, and barrel. Just go down on your knees and worship me, and they're yours."

Jesus' refusal was curt: "Beat it, Satan!" He backed his rebuke with a third quotation from Deuteronomy: "Worship the Lord your God, and only him. Serve him with absolute single-heartedness."

The Test was over. The Devil left. And in his place, angels! Angels came and took care of Jesus' needs.[1]

Jesus was *prepared* for his test, and he passed that test by *speaking the Word*. And then on day 41, he *launched* his epic ministry.

Now that you are prepared to make the most of your opportunity, it's time to proclaim your victory by vocalizing the promises found in Scripture. Something happens when we declare the Word of God. In the book of Daniel, chapter 9, I love that when Gabriel shows up to address Daniel's vision, he announces, "I'm here in response to your *words*."[2] He also made it clear that when Daniel first prayed, God's answer was set in motion! From Daniel's limited perspective, the answer didn't show up until 21 days later, but it was launched the moment Daniel opened his mouth.

> It's time to proclaim your victory by vocalizing the promises found in Scripture. Something happens when we declare the Word of God.

LAUNCHED

A few months ago, my family stayed overnight at a hotel that included a massive indoor water park. My 10-year-old daughter, Savannah, and I climbed the five flights of stairs to partake of waterslide bliss. A pair of enclosed tube slides protruded through the building walls, sending riders outside the hotel before circling back around inside. But the fastest and "funnest" slide—as my daughter would say—was shaped like a giant funnel and required the riders to sit in a one- or two-person inner tube.

My seven-year-old son, Ashton, watched from a distance as we screamed in excitement. He was missing out, and he knew it.

"Dad, I want to go with you guys!"

So off we went again, racing up the stairs. (And by that I mean they raced and I dragged myself.) Once we got to the top, the waterslide worker measured Ashton—who had to stand on his tiptoes—and we barely received the green light to ride. Savannah was tall enough to ride by herself, so off she went, screaming as if she had just won front-row tickets to see Taylor Swift.

"We're next!" I said excitedly. But just as we were about to climb into the two-person inner tube, Ashton changed his mind about riding.

"Oh no!" his compassionate father said. "You are riding, buddy! I just climbed five flights of stairs, and the only way down is in this tube!"

After some back-and-forth arguing and repeated reassurances that the ride wasn't that fast and he had nothing to worry about (which of course was a lie), I forced him to get on and off we went.

We shot through the first tunnel like two bats out of hell and whirled up into the funnel. As we headed toward the final chute, the raft slowed down and gently spun around in circles as if we were being sucked up into a giant drain. The worst was over—at least, Ashton hoped so.

Just as we were about to be suctioned into the chute, our raft spun quickly and unexpectedly in reverse. *Whoosh!* We flew backward down the slide like a plane coming in for a landing. As we approached the splash pool at slightly less than warp speed, Ashton looked at me as if to say, *I will never trust you again.*

Splash!

We hit the water like a meteorite colliding with Earth. My butt took the brunt of the impact, but because I'm so much heavier than Ashton, the downward force of my weight launched him into the air as if he'd been shot out of a circus cannon.

Nooooooo!

As I was flipping backward toward the water, I reached up as high as I could, hoping to catch him or at least grab a hand or foot to yank him down.

Not a chance.

He somersaulted out of control and smacked the water upside down. I flopped out of our raft as fast as I could to rescue him. As I jerked him out of the water, I hoisted him above my head and shouted, "Wasn't that awesome?"

Not a chance.

My wife didn't think it was all that awesome either.

Just as I launched my son toward his destiny, we need to launch our dreams and desires into motion. Okay, maybe not exactly as I launched my son, but you get the idea. To launch our dreams, we must boldly proclaim the Word of God, just as Jesus did.

Cry out to God.

Speak to your mountain.

Confess with your mouth.

Proclaim the truth of God's Word.

Shout to God with a voice of triumph.

No, I'm not talking about a "name-it-and-claim-it, blab-it-and-grab-it" gospel. I'm talking about praying audacious prayers backed up with the Word of God.

This is the sixth key to holding on and standing strong until your 41 comes: *Word up!*

Keys to help you hold on when life gets tough and stand strong until a new day dawns	1. *Know your enemy.* 2. *Embrace your cause.* 3. *Smash fear in the mouth.* 4. *Shake off doubts and doubters.* 5. *Prepare in order to receive a payoff.* 6. *Word up!*

"'Does not my word burn like fire?' says the LORD. 'Is it not like a mighty hammer that smashes a rock to pieces?'"[3]

When you *Word up*, you unleash an explosion of unmatched power. Jesus said that his words are Spirit and life. When a Roman officer approached Jesus with a request to heal his young, paralyzed servant, Jesus said, "I will come and heal him."

> But the officer said, "Lord, I am not worthy to have you come into my home. Just *say the word* from where you are, and my servant will be healed. I know this because I am under the authority of my superior officers, and I have authority over my soldiers. I only need to say, 'Go,' and they go, or 'Come,' and they come. And if I say to my slaves, 'Do this,' they do it."
>
> When Jesus heard this, he was amazed.[4]

Faith + declaring the Word of God = Word up! (#BoomGoesTheDynamite)

BRING THE BOOM!

It's imperative to feed yourself the Word of God—to place the Word inside yourself so that it will come out of you. If you make a practice of reading, studying, and memorizing Scripture, it will be there when you need it most. Whatever you put in is going to come out. Garbage in, garbage out— Word in, Word out. (#WordUp!)

Back to David. Goliath's words stirred him to action. He smashed fear in the mouth by accepting a challenge that everyone else had refused. He knocked down negativity and pushed past words of doubt. As he walked through the valley and finally stepped onto the battlefield, he was prepared and fueled up with courageous faith. Perhaps this

> If you make a practice of reading, studying, and memorizing Scripture, it will be there when you need it most.

is where David found the words he penned in the Psalms: "Even though I walk *through the valley* of the shadow of death, I will fear no evil."[5] Battles are often fought and won in the valley.

Are you in the valley right now? You don't have to stay there. Word up! Fight!

Goliath could not believe what he saw. "Am I a dog, that you come at me with a stick?"[6] he roared at David.

Am I getting punked?

Goliath thought it was some kind of lame joke because he thought David himself was a joke. The Bible says he cursed David by the names of his gods.

"Come over here, and I'll give your flesh to the birds and wild animals!"[7]

David shrugged it off.

Haters gonna hate.

Doubters gonna doubt.

Giants gonna fall.

With his slingshot locked and loaded, David was ready for a little smack talk of his own. And he was ready to back it up.

"You come to me with sword, spear, and javelin, but—"[8]

I learned long ago from my friend and mentor Eastman Curtis that when you see the word *but* in a sentence, you may as well throw out whatever words came before it. For example, when you apologize to your friend by saying, "I'm sorry I called you an idiot, but I cannot believe you dropped my phone in the lake," your *but* just negated your apology.

Sometimes we use our "buts" as an excuse. "I would join you on your 5K run, but I think I have to do something else that day." In David's case, he was about to diminish every last word Goliath had just said—and replace them with some words of his own. This was not an attempt to one-up Goliath. He was about to *Word-up* Goliath!

"You come to me with sword, spear, and javelin, *but—*"

I don't care.

That ain't nothing.

Whatever, dude . . .

"—but I come to you in the name of the Lord of Heaven's Armies—the God of the armies of Israel, whom you have defied."[9]

Goliath's taunts rolled off David's back because he knew what he was about to do. He already envisioned it. He was already prepared for it. And more than anything, God himself—the Lord of Heaven's Armies, the God of Israel, the God whom Goliath had just insulted—was about to back David up! Word up, baby!

David was about to bring the boom sauce.

Perhaps the enemy has lied to you. Maybe he has mocked you with confidence-shaking messages that resonate in a shaky self-image.

You're not good enough. You don't have what it takes. You'll never get through med school. Your wife will never forgive you. Your husband will never love you. Your kids will never serve God. You'll never get your business off the ground. You'll never quit drinking. You will never be used by God. You'll never get married. You'll never have kids. You'll never get a publishing deal. You'll never get healed. You'll never experience restoration. The list goes on and on and on.

David showed up ready to fight, but he wasn't fighting in his own strength and wisdom. God, the ultimate corner man, was backing him up.

What are you supposed to do? What are you supposed to say? Add "but God" to the sentence! Word up! Fight! Proclaim the Word of God! Bring the boom sauce!

David showed up ready to fight, but he wasn't fighting in his own strength and wisdom. God, the ultimate corner man, was backing him up.

News flash: God is backing *you* up!

I love what David said next. He told Goliath specifically what he was going to do to him and how he was going to do it: "Today the LORD will conquer you, and I will kill you and cut off your head. And then I will give the dead bodies of your men to the birds and wild animals, and the whole world will know that there is a God in Israel!"[10]

Can you imagine what the rest of the army of Israel was thinking when they heard David say this? First of all, it doesn't matter what they were thinking! Shake it off, right? They could have been excited that somebody was finally going to fight the giant, but my guess is they probably felt sorry for David. They probably had thoughts similar to those of the rest of the world when the United States hockey team was about to play Russia for the gold medal in the 1980 Olympics. That's why that game was called the "Miracle on Ice." The Israelites were probably trying to talk sense into him: "David, get back here, bro! You're going to get killed. You're going to mess things up for everybody!"

I also love how David ended his declaration: "And the whole world will know that there is a God in Israel!"

Boom! God was about to show up and show off his stuff— and he was going to use the most unlikely person.

He did it with David. Why not with you? Why not with me?

Bible scholars and historians believe that David was about 17 years old when he killed Goliath. Don't you just love his confidence? I mean, it's almost cockiness, right? And yet it's not. David was 100 percent confident *in God*. And it was that audacious faith that fueled his willingness to decree what he was about to do.

> You will delight in the Almighty
> And lift up your face to God.
> You will pray to Him, and He will hear you; . . .
> You will also decree a thing, and it will be established
>   for you;
> And light will shine on your ways.[11]

If we really believe what the Word of God says, we should be willing to speak it.

> Submit to God, and you will have peace;
>   then things will go well for you.
> Listen to his instructions,
>   and store them in your heart.
> If you return to the Almighty, you will be restored—
>   so clean up your life. . . .
> Then you will take delight in the Almighty
>   and look up to God.
> You will pray to him, and he will hear you,
>   and you will fulfill your vows to him.
> You will succeed in whatever you choose to do,
>   and light will shine on the road ahead of you.[12]

That's good stuff right there.

I'm inspired by the boldness of this quote from a Joel Osteen devotional: "I declare I will put actions behind my faith. I will not be passive or indifferent. I will demonstrate my faith by taking bold steps to move toward what God has put in my heart."[13]

That is exactly what David did. The very moment he stepped onto the battlefield, he put his faith on display before both armies. The prophet Daniel says, "The people who know their God shall be strong, and carry out great exploits."[14] Another translation of this verse says, "The people who know their God shall stand firm and take action."[15]

Are you willing to take action?

Believe it.

Say it.

Do it.

DEFEATING THE SNAKE

I know from personal experience that taking action is much easier to talk about than to actually do. I haven't always done the best job of backing up what I believe. Growing up in church, surrounded by ministry, can make you susceptible to responding like a robot. It's good to be taught to speak words of life, but if those words aren't backed up with faith, they are just idle chatter.

When a crisis shows up unannounced and we find ourselves in the middle of a storm, that's when we really find out what we believe.

When a crisis shows up unannounced and we find ourselves in the middle of a storm, that's when we really find out what we believe.

When my wife was pregnant with our son, Ashton, my

friend Keith approached me to share a vision he'd had. He had seen an image of my wife with a snake wrapped around her stomach—"horizontally, like a pool floaty."

I prayed protection over my wife and son and filed away the memory of Keith's words.

On October 24, 2007, Annette went into labor, and we almost didn't make it to the hospital in time. At 2:51 a.m., I dropped her off in the emergency room circle drive, parked the car, and sprinted inside.

Annette was filling out paperwork.

Finally, they brought her a wheelchair and I began steering her along the hallway. Things were more serious than anyone had originally realized—her contractions were only a minute apart, and she was almost fully dilated when they got her to the room—and apparently I was moving too slowly because an attendant pushed me out of the way, grabbed the handles of the wheelchair, and began darting down the hall. Within minutes of getting Annette into a bed and prepping everything, we had a baby.

Ashton Richie Tate entered this world lifeless at 3:32 a.m. The umbilical cord was wrapped around his neck three times, and he wasn't breathing. He was pale and limp.

Remember Keith's vision? I was completely gripped with fear. Annette knew immediately that something was wrong when she didn't hear Ashton cry and the nurses whisked him away. It was the scariest moment of our lives.

Word up, right? I began to pray out loud and speak words of life over our little boy, and I didn't care who heard me.

It just so happened that one of our friends was the on-call

doctor on that overnight shift. Initially, Annette hadn't wanted him in the room, for reasons that you can understand. But he was also the best OB-GYN in that hospital, which is why God had him there at that exact moment.

After being notified of our situation, he ran down the hall and into our room to resuscitate Ashton. He saved Ashton's life, pure and simple. Never had I been so happy to hear a baby cry. We prayed. We claimed the Lord's promises. We trusted. And God rescued.

I don't know if you've done the math, but from the moment I dropped Annette off until the moment when Ashton entered the world, it was exactly 41 minutes! I'll admit I'm stunned by that because Annette and I didn't calculate those minutes until just now as we were reviewing this story for the book. I have no words—just streaming tears and a grateful heart at the realization that Ashton will forever be our "41 will come" miracle.

FAITH AND FOOLISHNESS

The story doesn't end there. Our doctors informed us that Ashton had a broken clavicle. We were just thankful he was alive, but a few hours later, our friend, Dr. Boyd, sat us down to inform us that the situation was more serious than they had originally thought.

"Due to the trauma of Ashton's stressful birth—by the way, if his umbilical cord had not been wrapped around his neck, he would have been born in the car—we believe he suffered what's called a brachial plexus injury."

We've never heard of that. Is it bad? What's going on?

According to the Mayo Clinic website, a brachial plexus injury is an injury to "the network of nerves that sends signals from your spine to your shoulder, arm and hand. . . . Injury occurs when these nerves are stretched, compressed, or . . . torn. . . . Damage to . . . the brachial plexus tends to occur when your shoulder is forced down while your neck stretches up and away from the injured shoulder."[16]

What does all that mean? Ashton had no mobility in his right arm. After a slew of questions from us, Dr. Boyd said he was encouraged that Ashton could move his fingers—but it still wasn't a guarantee that he would have movement in his arm—ever.

> As Solomon says in Proverbs, "Death and life are in the power of the tongue." Our words can bring death, or they can bring life.

That *ever* landed with the force of a punch to the gut and left us numb. In a matter of hours, we had traveled through the valley of the shadow of death, up the mountain, and then back down into the valley.

We were faced with an important decision: Do we speak words of life or words of doubt? As Solomon says in Proverbs, "Death and life are in the power of the tongue."[17] Our words can bring death, or they can bring life. In *The Message*, Eugene Peterson renders Solomon's words this way: "Words kill, words give life; they're either poison or fruit—you choose."

We decided then and there that we were going to Word up and trust *Jehovah Rapha*—God our Healer. We would speak faith, decree faith, and declare faith.

Ashton will move that arm. It doesn't matter what the doctors

say. We serve the Great Physician. If God is the one who fash-
ioned our son in Annette's womb, then he can breathe life back
into Ashton's nerves.

Allow me to clarify that I am not against doctors. I'm
not going to tell you to throw away your meds and defy
your physician's orders. There's a fine line between faith and
foolishness. Use discernment. God uses doctors. He gives
physicians and surgeons the skill to treat the human body
in remarkable ways. He gives scientists and engineers the
wisdom to create technology and pharmaceuticals that have
helped to heal millions of people.

I'm a perfect example. I wear hearing aids, and I thank God
for that technology. It would be foolish of me to throw away
my hearing aids simply because I believe that God can breathe
life back into my ears. God could heal me at any moment
(because Jesus has already paid the price of my healing), but
until that manifestation comes, I'm going to take advantage of
the latest technology. That's not a lack of faith. I thank God for
doctors, nurses, and everyone in the medical field.

I'm also not suggesting that we can declare any outcome
we desire and it will be so. When I say, "Word up!" I mean
that we plumb the depths of Scripture for God's promises,
we speak his Word back to him in faith, and we trust his
wisdom, mercy, and grace for the outcome.

Ashton was referred to Easter Seals, a national organization that assists families of children with disabilities and
special needs, but before we could even leave the hospital,
the devil used one of our nurses to shake our faith. She told
Annette and me that her teenage son had a brachial plexus

injury and he had never regained movement in his arm. She was pretty intense. We explained that our doctor was encouraged that Ashton could move his fingers, but she shot down every ounce of hope we had. It was as if she didn't want our son to be healed because her son hadn't been. She was a hardcore Negative Nellie, and I'll be honest with you: It rattled us. Perhaps she meant well. I'm sure she had no idea the enemy was using her to deter us from believing for a miracle. But we had to Word up, shake it off, and refuel our faith.

We immediately began taking Ashton to Easter Seals for occupational therapy, even though he was only a few days old. Karen, his occupational therapist, was awesome. She worked with him twice a week, and we continued speaking the Word of God over him.

We have a relationship with the Great Physician. *Word up.*

Unfortunately, things didn't get better. They got worse. After a few months with Easter Seals, Ashton was referred to St. Louis Children's Hospital. Though it was hard to hear, "Ashton's not really responding the way we want him to," we were encouraged when they told us that one of the best brachial plexus physicians in the world was at St. Louis Children's. I couldn't help but whisper under my breath, *And we have a relationship with the Great Physician.* Word up.

We arrived in St. Louis with high expectations, but left feeling as if we'd been kicked in the gut—again. Proverbs says, "Hope deferred makes the heart sick."[18] Yep. I can vouch for that.

Ashton's prognosis was not good. A neurosurgeon sat us

down and said, "Your son will most likely need surgery. If he ever regains movement, it's probable that he won't have full range of motion above shoulder height." Then he added, "You will need to educate yourselves on what it's like to raise a child with brachial plexus." That was more than a crushing blow. It was a reality check. The thought that Ashton would not be able to throw a baseball with his right arm paralyzed me. I vividly remember thumbing through the brachial plexus pamphlets next to my wife with a knot in my throat, looking for the barest shred of hope. We were encouraged to see pictures of young boys, girls, and teenagers living completely normal lives with immobile limbs. Still, we left that day determined to accept nothing less than complete healing. Word up.

In the meantime, we continued taking Ashton to Easter Seals while waiting for his next appointment in St. Louis. And we prayed—a lot. We thanked God that Ashton was alive. And we thanked God for healing him, even though we couldn't see it yet with our natural eyes. Yes, it was scary. But courage is walking on water even when you're freaked out of your mind. We kept speaking to our storm. And Ashton began to improve. "Hope deferred makes the heart sick, *but a longing fulfilled is a tree of life*."[19] Ashton's brachial branches began to stir. Go, God!

A few months later, we returned to St. Louis Children's Hospital. This time, after the neurosurgeon examined Ashton and reviewed his X-rays, he sat Annette and me down and said, "Your son does not need surgery. Keep sending him to Easter Seals until they release him, but you don't have to bring him back here. I believe he's going to be fine."

We shed tears of gratitude and joy.

Eventually, Easter Seals released Ashton completely. Today, he plays baseball. He plays basketball. He's slightly obsessed with Minecraft. He occasionally helps me preach—and guess which arm he uses to hold the microphone? His right arm, because he's right-handed.

Boom goes the dynamite!

USE YOUR FAITH

The morning after Jesus "borrowed" a donkey and made his triumphant entry into Jerusalem, he and his disciples were leaving town again. Jesus was hungry.

> He noticed a fig tree in full leaf a little way off, so he went over to see if he could find any figs. But there were only leaves because it was too early in the season for fruit. Then Jesus said to the tree, "May no one ever eat your fruit again!" And the disciples heard him say it.[20]

I love this story. Jesus killed a tree because he was hungry and the tree had no fruit. I guess it's safe to say that he was not a tree hugger. (Hey, don't be mad at me. Jesus did it.)

Okay, there really is a lesson here. Let's pick up the story a few verses later:

> The next morning as they passed by the fig tree [Jesus] had cursed, the disciples noticed it had withered from the roots up. Peter remembered what Jesus had said

to the tree on the previous day and exclaimed, "Look, Rabbi! The fig tree you cursed has withered and died!"

Then Jesus said to the disciples, "Have faith in God. I tell you the truth, you can say to this mountain, 'May you be lifted up and thrown into the sea,' and it will happen. But you must really believe it will happen and have no doubt in your heart. I tell you, you can pray for anything, and if you believe that you've received it, it will be yours. But when you are praying, first forgive anyone you are holding a grudge against, so that your Father in heaven will forgive your sins, too."[21]

I hope you understand that this chapter is about so much more than simply speaking positive words. I am talking about speaking the Word of God and mixing it with faith! David believed God. He knew God was going to see him through. That's the difference. He wasn't merely hoping he could pull off a victory against all odds. He didn't randomly decide to talk some smack to Goliath. He spoke with authority and confidence because he believed in God and in what he was saying. Jesus says, "I tell you, you can pray for anything, and if you believe that you've received it, it will be yours."[22]

Every one of us has been given a measure of faith. Let's use it!

SPEAK TO YOUR STORM

I have another story to tell you about a time when a fierce storm showed up out of nowhere and assaulted my family, but first, what does Jesus say about unannounced storms?

> As evening came, Jesus said to his disciples, "Let's cross to the other side of the lake." So they took Jesus in the boat and started out, leaving the crowds behind (although other boats followed). But soon a fierce storm came up. High waves were breaking into the boat, and it began to fill with water.
>
> Jesus was sleeping at the back of the boat with his head on a cushion. The disciples woke him up, shouting, "Teacher, don't you care that we're going to drown?"
>
> When Jesus woke up, he rebuked the wind and said to the waves, "Silence! Be still!" Suddenly the wind stopped, and there was a great calm. Then he asked them, "Why are you afraid? Do you still have no faith?"[23]

Have you been there? You're enjoying life, heading toward your next destination, when suddenly a storm shows up. The wind starts to rock your boat, the water rushes in, and you feel as if you're about to go under. A sinking feeling is a scary feeling. So what are you supposed to do at that moment? Word up. Speak to the storm!

The disciples could have done that, but instead they woke up Jesus. My favorite part of this story is that Jesus was sleeping. That's what I call true peace amid the storm. My dad jokes that Jesus was probably sleeping with one eye open—to see whether the disciples were going to do something about the storm. And they could have. But they didn't. After Jesus calmed the storm, he reminded them of that.

A few years ago, I attended a conference at NewSpring Church in Anderson, South Carolina, and Judah Smith was one of the speakers. He preached a powerful message called "In the Middle of the Meantime." I'll never forget the impact of that message. "What do you do when you're in the middle of a storm in the middle of a lake? *Stay in the boat.* Why? *Because Jesus is in the boat with you.*"

You are not alone. Speak to your storm! (#WordUp)

SEVEN-WEEK STORM

On September 1, 2009, my 61-year-old mom, Karen, was sent home from her local hospital with pneumonia. No big deal. Pneumonia *can* be very serious, but her doctors weren't overly concerned.

Two days later, *I* was the one who was concerned. I remember talking to Mom on the phone, and she just didn't sound right.

"I'm coming to get you," I said, "and we're going to OSF." Saint Francis Medical Center in Peoria is the largest and most highly respected hospital in our region.

Upon arriving at the ER, Mom was rushed into an exam room to see whether she was having a heart attack. It turned out to be pericarditis—an inflammation of the lining surrounding the heart. The doctors told me they would treat her with antibiotics, and it was probable that Mom would be released in a couple of days.

By Sunday morning, I was slightly concerned that Mom had not yet been released. After calling her on my way to church, I was fairly certain she wasn't going home that day either—unless she made an instant turnaround.

Hmm, I don't like the way she sounds. The doctor said it would be two days—this is the third day, and it seems like she's getting worse.

After church, Annette, the kids, and I went straight to the hospital to check on Mom and give Dad some company. The kids were excited to see Nanny and Poppy, but Mom appeared weak and lethargic—a little too sluggish and soft-spoken for my liking.

Throughout the afternoon, I noticed that Mom's body temperature seemed to be dropping. Her skin was alarmingly cold—enough so that I notified a nurse: "Her skin is freezing! This can't be normal."

I don't remember what the nurse's response was after she checked Mom's temperature, but I know I wasn't satisfied.

What is going on?

Savannah (almost five years old at the time) and Ashton (almost two) were getting antsy and hungry, so I walked them and Annette to the parking deck so they could leave. As I trekked back across the hospital to the cardiac wing, I prayed, but I still had a nagging feeling that something wasn't right. When I stepped off the elevator on the fifth floor, I noticed doctors and nurses running toward the hall where my mom's room was located, and the Code Blue alarm was ringing loudly.

No! It can't be Mom!

As soon as I rounded the corner, the nightmare became a reality. I rushed frantically into Mom's room, where I found 18 medical personnel trying to save her life. Dad was wedged in the corner, praying fervently. I could tell by the look on everyone's faces that hope had left the room. We were about to lose Mom.

God, please do something!

After quietly pleading with God to do something, I knew that *I* had to do something. Practice what you preach, right?

Okay, it's go time! Life or death.

Like a quarterback charging to the middle of the huddle, I plowed my way through the doctors and nurses. At that moment, I didn't care about protocol or consequences. My mom needed a miracle and I had the same Holy Spirit inside of me that had raised Christ from the dead.

After shouldering my way through the tangle of medical professionals, I placed my hand on Mom's body and prayed with boldness and bravery.

"In the name of *Jesus*—" I shouted. I don't remember what else I prayed, but I know it was short, to the point, and loud. Mom sat up almost instantly and began projectile vomiting. (Sorry to be so descriptive, but at the time this was a *great* thing.) Mom was then transferred to the intensive care unit, where she was listed as "critical but stable."

When I recalled this moment recently with my mom, she told me that her mind had been alert while all of this was happening, but she had no control over her body. When she coded, she saw the faces of her grandchildren—my kids and my sister's daughter, Jadealynn—and she prayed to God, *I want to live. I want to see my grandchildren grow up.* She told me that right after she prayed that, I ran over and laid hands on her. Amazing.

We thought the worst was over, but it was only beginning. I pretty much lived at the hospital for the next six weeks. Mom had a rampant infection around her heart, and the physicians and surgeons were having a difficult time identifying it. This made it extremely challenging to find the right antibiotic to treat the infection. The next month and a half was an emotional roller coaster that included mountains of hope and valleys of despair, prayer without ceasing, and lots of tears. It also included chest tubes, ventilators, and multiple surgeries to drain fluid. Mom spent at least two of those weeks in the ICU in a medically induced coma.

During one of her surgeries, I remember sitting in the family waiting room, working on my laptop, when an attendant approached me. She quietly tapped me on the shoulder and told me that a priest was on the phone and wanted to talk to me. OSF is a Catholic hospital, so priests double as chaplains. My heart was instantly gripped with fear. My last encounter with a priest at that hospital had come 11 years earlier, when my wife and I were informed that her father had passed away upon arrival.

"I just wanted to let you know that your mom is doing fine," he said. And I have no idea what he said next.

Are you trying to give me a heart attack?

After that phone call, I decided to get out of the ICU

waiting room, where doom and gloom hung like a heavy curtain. I'd had enough. I decided to hang out in the cafeteria when I wasn't in Mom's room.

Another time when Mom was about to have surgery, my dad and I went to pray with her in the surgery preparation room. As she was about to be rolled away, someone came charging into the room to call off the surgery. A nurse had forgotten to note on Mom's chart that she was on a blood thinner. Had they gone through with the surgery, she probably would have bled out.

Up and down. Back and forth. Word up.

One day while Dad and I were in the cafeteria eating, we received a call from one of Mom's doctors, who needed to speak with us. We were not prepared for that conversation.

"Karen is very sick. She has a widespread infection. She is septic. Her organs are shutting down. You need to contact the rest of your family."

I was broken. One of Mom's friends from work came to say good-bye. But I refused to go there in my mind.

I remember breaking down and calling Annette, my two siblings, a cousin, and some close friends. After I got off the phone, my dad and I went into Mom's room to pray for a miracle.

"You need to get a minister," the nurse said to my dad.

"Chuck and I are both ministers," Dad replied.

But as I looked down at my mom's sedated body—a maze of tubes, wires, and cables—I realized I had nothing left. I couldn't pray. I tried, but all I could do was weep. I looked at my dad and said, "You pray."

My dad is an old-school power preacher, and in that moment he prayed as if he were Elijah calling down fire on Mount Carmel.

After Dad's audacious prayer, one of the nurses said to me, "I have never heard anyone ever pray like that before."

God heard. God responded. Mom defied death once again, and this time she began to improve.

Eventually, Mom was moved out of the ICU and began taking steps toward regaining her health and strength. She needed one last minor surgery, but the prognosis was for a full recovery.

When they took her in for the final surgery, my family and I waited downstairs. They gave me a pager and said they would notify me when Mom was in recovery.

We waited.

We waited and waited.

We waited some more.

Why is this taking so long?

Two hours after the time when the surgery should have ended, the pager died.

Sheesh! What is going on?

Finally, an attendant emerged from the elevator and told me that one of the doctors wanted to meet with me. As I rode the elevator upstairs to see him, all I could pray was, "Come on, God. You didn't bring us this far to have it end badly, did you?"

On the surgery floor, I was greeted by the anesthesiologist.

"Your mom coded in the recovery room," he said

matter-of-factly. After a short pause that felt like an eternity, he added, "But we were able to resuscitate her. She's going to have to go back into the ICU for a couple of days—which means she'll have to be intubated again—but we expect her to begin her road to recovery after that."

I thanked him, we shook hands, and he walked away.

Then I lost it.

Mom began rehab shortly after her release from the ICU, and on October 20 she was discharged from the hospital— almost seven weeks after being admitted. Before leaving the hospital, Mom said to one of her doctors, "Thank you for saving my life."

"Thank you for allowing me to be a part of your amazing recovery," he replied.

One of her other doctors calls her "the Miracle Woman," and rightly so. There is absolutely no other explanation. (By the way, this is another miracle, and another story for another time, but Mom's hospital bill was paid in full!)

(#BoomGoesTheDynamite)

Five weeks after being released from the hospital, Mom went back to full-time work with the help of a walker. That was more than six years ago, and her recovery has been complete. Today, she's retired and serves on the greeting team at our church. Recently, I watched a broadcast of a live worship service at our church, and there was Mom on the front row, worshiping with her arms outstretched as the band rocked on. I couldn't help but rejoice as the tears streamed down my face.

Here's what I've learned: If you will stand on the promises of God during your storm, you will still be standing when the sun comes out again.

_____

#41WillCome
#WordUp
#BoomGoesTheDynamite

RECKLESS CHARGE

When Goliath started forward, David ran toward him.
1 SAMUEL 17:48, CEV

*It's good to feel stupid sometimes and do things
that are out of your comfort zone.*
MARY-LOUISE PARKER

THERE'S A STORY of a man who rode into a western town on
a stagecoach. He was soon hired as a bartender at the local
saloon.

"There's only one thing you need to know," the bar owner
told him. "If you ever hear that Big John is coming to town,
drop everything you're doing and run for your life!"

Things went fine for several months. The bartender never
heard any mention of Big John—that is, until one day when
a big, strong cowhand with a ghost-white face burst through
the swinging doors shouting, "Big John's a-comin'! Big John's
a-comin'!"

The patrons scrambled for the door, knocking the bartender to the floor and running over him as they rushed to
safety. In their haste, some even dove out the windows.

As the bartender got up from the floor, dusted himself

off, and gathered his senses, a giant of a man burst through the saloon doors, riding bareback on a buffalo and using a rattlesnake for a whip. He flung the snake into the corner and knocked over several tables as he made his way up to the bar. Slamming his huge fist down onto the bar and splitting it in half, he yelled, "Give me a drink!"

"Y-y-y-y-yes, sir!" said the frightened bartender.

The man bit the top off the bottle with his teeth and downed the contents in a single gulp. Letting out a massive belch that shattered the saloon mirror, he quickly turned to leave.

The bartender stuttered, "W-w-w-would you like another d-d-drink?"

"I ain't got time!" the man roared as he jumped back onto his buffalo and retrieved his snake. "Big John's a-comin'!"

SPIRITUAL STAMPEDE

We've all had times when we've felt like the bartender in the story. Frantic. Shaking. Scared out of our minds. But now we have learned how to smash fear in the mouth. Like David, we have stepped onto the battlefield. What next?

David had two options as he faced off against Goliath: defense or offense.

Israel had been playing defense for 40 days. On day 41, David chose offense. David didn't crouch behind his shield and hide. He didn't stumble backward and retreat. He didn't run in circles and dance around like Floyd Mayweather. He ran *toward* Goliath.

One day when I was a kid at summer camp, I was running from a group of girls. (Okay, for that statement alone, I should surrender my man card. It was probably the same year I slapped that dude in a fight.) I was enjoying the chase and decided that I would escape and impress them at the same time by jumping from a boulder about 10 feet high to a tree branch about five feet away. What I didn't know was that the tree branch was dead. (You know where this is going, right?) As soon as my hands hit the branch, it snapped, and I landed on my back on the ground. The impact knocked the wind out of me—along with whatever was left of my dignity. I ended up with bruised ribs, a bruised ego, and no girlfriend.

Moral of the story: *Don't run away.*

When David ran at Goliath, he brought everything he had! It was a reckless charge—a spiritual stampede, if you will. And this audacious attack has ignited hope in underdogs ever since.

This is our seventh key to holding on and standing strong until your 41 comes: *Attack!*

Keys to help you hold on when life gets tough and stand strong until a new day dawns	*1. Know your enemy.* *2. Embrace your cause.* *3. Smash fear in the mouth.* *4. Shake off doubts and doubters.* *5. Prepare in order to receive a payoff.* *6. Word up!* *7. Attack!*

As you step out in faith to attack the giant standing between you and your victory, take confidence in the words of David: "In your strength I can crush an army; with my God I can scale any wall."[1]

It's time to fight!

GO BIG OR GO HOME

The moment that David placed one foot forward, there was no turning back. It was go big or go home! Are you prepared to take your leap of faith? Are you ready to charge forward? For the Israelites in the time of Moses, 40 years was a long time to wander in the wilderness. But their step of faith into the Jordan River (see Joshua 3) produced a promise that the previous generation had never had a chance to experience.

> Joshua and all the Israelites . . . arrived at the banks of the Jordan River, where they camped before crossing. Three days later the Israelite officers went through the camp, giving these instructions to the people: "When you see the Levitical priests carrying the Ark of the Covenant of the LORD your God, move out from your positions and follow them. Since you have never traveled this way before, they will guide you. Stay about half a mile behind them, keeping a clear distance between you and the Ark. Make sure you don't come any closer."[2]

The Ark of the Covenant contained the Ten Commandments. The Ark itself represented the very presence of God, so only the priests were permitted to handle it. This was a monumental moment. The people hadn't gone this way before. They'd been in the wilderness for 40 years. Now they were going a new way. They were getting ready to enter the Promised Land.

When traveling, I love exploring new routes. There's something exhilarating about discovering new landscape, scenery, and gas stations with clean restrooms. A few months ago, my family and I, along with Cory Vance, our church's youth pastor, took a road trip to Arizona to speak at a youth camp. It was our sixth consecutive year, so Cory suggested that we try a new route. Instead of driving through Missouri, Oklahoma, Texas, and New Mexico to get to Arizona, we decided to go through Iowa, Nebraska, Colorado, and Utah. Let me just say it's impossible to drive through Colorado and not recognize our Creator's handiwork.

So the Israelites followed the presence of God to the land he had promised they would inhabit. (This is a good opportunity to remind you to follow the Holy Spirit's leading, and to remind you that sometimes the only route to the Promised Land is through the wilderness. The question is, will you throw your faith out the window and gripe at God, or will you hold on to your faith and cling to God? Don't forget that God knows what he's doing and that his ways are better than yours.) When the Israelites got to the edge of the Promised Land, Joshua told them, "Purify yourselves, for tomorrow the LORD will do great wonders among you."[3]

> **Follow the Holy Spirit's leading. . . . Sometimes the only route to the Promised Land is through the wilderness.**

Tomorrow.

Can you imagine trying to fall asleep the night before you're about to experience a place that you've only heard about for your entire life? This would be somewhat similar—though certainly not in scope or importance—to taking your kids to Disney World for the first time, or perhaps to the Grand Canyon, Europe, Hawaii, the Alps, or Walmart.

(Walmart? Hey, it's all a matter of perspective. I have some relatives from Sweden who think it's hilarious that we're obsessed with IKEA, and yet when they visited us, they went straight to Walmart to take pictures.)

So the Israelites must have been stoked. They had to be absolutely pumped.

God used Moses to rescue the Israelites out of Egypt, but after they crossed through the Red Sea and entered the wilderness, they were told about a 40-year detour. Not 40 days. Not four years. But 40 *long* years.

Not only does hope deferred make the heart sick, but it also can give you a bad attitude. This is exactly what happened to the Israelites. Instead of being grateful for what they had, they complained about everything they didn't have. In fact, it was their bickering, whining, and complaining that earned them the extended desert time.

That's called foot-in-mouth disease. My kids catch it occasionally. It's one thing that my wife and I won't tolerate, and it's something God can't stand. Whining in the wilderness makes the wilderness wandering longer. It's kind of like when you tell your kids that they can't go outside to play until they clean their rooms, and then they argue with you for an hour before they finally give in. And you're thinking, *If you would have done what I said when I first said it, you could have been outside forty-five minutes ago!*

Yeah, it's a head-scratcher.

Even Moses messed up, and he didn't get to enter the Promised Land. That still bothers me and makes me want to do my best to live a life of obedience. Joshua was Moses' successor, and he had the honor and responsibility of leading God's people into the very land he had been privileged to glimpse as part of the advance team. But that was 40 years ago. Now they were finally going home. No more traveling. No more setting up camp every day. Their 40-year road trip was about to end. Their 41 was about to come!

At RockChurch, we got just a taste of that kind of lifestyle. We were mobile for our first nine years, renting space but never having our own. Set up. Tear down. Set up. Tear down. Put stuff in storage. Take it out. Load in. Load out. Get some great new leaders. Burn 'em out. Up and down and back and forth. Then we leased a storefront for two years. There was no more setting up and tearing down, but there were still challenges from not owning the property: shared parking, noise restrictions, and landlord issues. But after 11 years in 10 separate buildings, we finally purchased our own property. That was our 41.

Here, Israel was about to enter their 41. But there was one last obstacle.

Uh, isn't that a giant river?

The LORD told Joshua, "Today I will begin to make you a great leader in the eyes of all the Israelites.

> They will know that I am with you, just as I was
> with Moses. Give this command to the priests who
> carry the Ark of the Covenant: 'When you reach the
> banks of the Jordan River, take a few steps into the
> river and stop there.'"[4]

God will never ask you to do something that he won't equip
you to do—and he will always back you up. So remember,
if the Holy Spirit leads you to a river, he will make a way for
you to cross. But he usually waits for you to take the first step.

> Joshua told the Israelites, "Come and listen to what
> the LORD your God says. Today you will know that
> the living God is among you. He will surely drive
> out the Canaanites, Hittites, Hivites, Perizzites,
> Girgashites, Amorites, and Jebusites ahead of you.
> Look, the Ark of the Covenant, which belongs to
> the Lord of the whole earth, will lead you across the
> Jordan River!"[5]

Not only was God going to lead them on a reckless charge
into the Promised Land, but he was also going to knock out
their enemies in the process.

What is God asking you to step into? He's got you! He
already sees the outcome. He knows what's next. He's already
there. Go!

> Choose twelve men from the tribes of Israel, one
> from each tribe. The priests will carry the Ark of

the Lord, the Lord of all the earth. As soon as
their feet touch the water, the flow of water will be
cut off upstream, and the river will stand up like a
wall.[6]

Notice that God said that nothing would happen until the
priests' feet touched the water. Faith without works is dead,
right?[7] I would rather take a leap of faith into the unknown
than stand on the bank and watch everyone else. You can't
win if you don't play. You can't play if you don't step onto
the field. I'm in.

> So the people left their camp to cross the Jordan, and
> the priests who were carrying the Ark of the Covenant
> went ahead of them. It was the harvest season, and the
> Jordan was overflowing its banks. But as soon as the
> feet of the priests who were carrying the Ark touched
> the water at the river's edge, the water above that point
> began backing up a great distance away at a town
> called Adam, which is near Zarethan. And the water
> below that point flowed on to the Dead Sea until the
> riverbed was dry. Then all the people crossed over near
> the town of Jericho.
>   Meanwhile, the priests who were carrying the
> Ark of the Lord's Covenant stood on dry ground
> in the middle of the riverbed as the people passed
> by. They waited there until the whole nation of
> Israel had crossed the Jordan on dry ground.[8]

I've heard estimates that as many as 2.5 million people crossed through the river. Imagine the step of faith—the leap of faith—the 12 priests had to take! They had to step into the river at flood stage.

Have you ever been near a flood? According to a recent article in *The New Yorker*, "a grown man is knocked over by ankle-deep water moving at 6.7 miles an hour."[9] Common sense would dictate that you don't want to step into flood-waters. Still, that's what God had told the priests to do; the miracle was on their shoulders. Their obedience or disobedience would affect a lot of people, just as David's obedience to fight Goliath was so much more than a personal battle. His willingness to do something big affected an entire nation.

When I was in high school, my friend Rob and I went on an all-day float trip one hot summer day, down the Mackinaw River in a two-person inflatable raft. The Mackinaw runs through central Illinois and is fairly safe unless it swells or floods. When that happens, it can turn deadly in an instant, and it has claimed several lives over the years. We found out firsthand that the river can be tricky and can go from shallow to deep without warning. In fact, some spots were so shallow that we had to carry our raft, but we still had to keep an eye out for fast drop-offs.

Our adventure that day was mostly uneventful—minus a thunderstorm, Rob losing a shoe, me banging my knee on a rock, and both of us getting chased by bears. (Okay, we weren't really chased by bears.) We were scheduled to be picked up by Rob's mom at 4:00 p.m. at the third bridge.

Looking back, we should have nailed down which highway she would meet us at—not which bridge.

We reached our destination ahead of schedule and pulled the raft onto the bank to wait for our ride. Four o'clock came and went while we waited and waited and waited. This was a time before anyone had cell phones, so there was nothing we could do but wait.

During our downtime, Rob remembered that his mom had mentioned that one of the bridges along the Mackinaw had been torn down. But then we met some people who told us that no bridges had been torn down along that stretch— which meant we had stopped one bridge too soon and Rob's mom was most likely waiting for us at the *next* bridge.

In hindsight, we should have walked up to the highway and flagged down a ride. But we didn't think of that. Instead, we put the raft back in the water and headed for the next bridge. Distance: unknown. Speed of river: unknown.

Fast-forward five hours. It was 9:00 p.m. and plenty dark by the time we finally arrived at the correct bridge. Not a lot of streetlights along the river. But as we approached in our raft, we could see a lot of flashing lights. Either there had been a big accident or we were in big trouble.

Well, there wasn't an accident, and we weren't in trouble— because everyone was too elated to see us alive. The authorities had already sent out a search-and-rescue team, and they were about to send out a search plane or a helicopter. Everyone had assumed that the river had swelled and claimed two more lives.

At the crossing of the Jordan, the priests didn't sit on

their hands near the river's edge and say, "We're just going to believe that God will do this. If he wants us to cross, he will transport us over." They knew they had to act.

But this was a scary moment because the banks were flooded. Joshua also says that the water backed upstream to a town called Adam—about 20 miles away. Some historians believe that it took hours before the water actually parted— which means that the priests would have had to stand in the water for a while. They would have had to stand there waiting and trusting God. But regardless of whether it parted immediately or took two hours, the bottom line is that God performed a miracle because of the priests' faith and obedience.

WATER WALKER

One of my favorite stories in the New Testament is the familiar passage in which Jesus walks on water. Of course, my favorite part of the story is not that Jesus walked on water, but that Peter did too.

It was late at night—about three o'clock in the morning— on a dark and stormy night that produced rough waters. All of the disciples were in a boat, battling the heavy waves, when Jesus came walking on the water and scared the living daylights out of them! They thought he was a ghost. Jesus responded by saying, "Don't be afraid. . . . Take courage. I am here!"[10]

All of the disciples, except Peter, must have been thinking, *Are you kidding me?*

I love Peter's faith. He said, "Lord, if it's really you, tell me to come to you, walking on the water."[11]

And Jesus said, "Come on, man! Let's go!"[12]

Peter stepped out of the boat and walked on water.

The priests stepped into the Jordan River and the waters parted.

David stepped onto the battlefield and slew the giant.

When God says, "Step out," giants fall.

When God says, "Step out," waters part.

When God says, "Step out," gravity and surface tension are irrelevant.

When God says, "Step out," miracles happen.

Peter got out of the boat and walked on water while the rest of the disciples sat and watched. Are you watching someone else walk on water, or is someone watching you? Are you in the boat or out on the lake? Poor Peter always gets ripped for sinking, but he was the only one with enough faith to step out of the boat in the first place!

> Your destiny requires faith. It requires trust. It requires courage. It requires Jesus. And it requires a steady heart.

There were 11 other dudes who could have been out on that water. But only one guy was.

I want to be like Peter!

At a recent Re:Write Conference, author James Rubart asked a challenging question: "When are you going to step out of the shadows and into the destiny God has created for you?"

Your destiny requires faith.

It requires trust.

It requires courage.

It requires Jesus.

And it requires a steady heart

Peter wasn't out on the water for long before he lost his focus and began to sink.

David kept his focus true and killed Goliath.

FOCUS

Peter lost focus because he became distracted. If the devil can't defeat you by getting you to succumb to obvious temptations, he will try to distract you to get your eyes off Jesus.

A few years ago, as I drove past a golf course on my way to the church on a beautiful Sunday morning, I saw a couple of guys playing the hole closest to the highway. One of them was getting ready to drive the ball from the edge of the well-manicured fairway.

He settled over his shot and prepared to hit the fire out of the ball. But just as he entered his downswing, I hammered my car horn as hard as I could. The timing was so impeccable that I still can't quite believe it. I drove by that golf course every week, and I had always thought about blasting my horn, but this time I followed through with my childish mischief.

Not only did I scare the life out of him—his club kicked up more grass than my lawn mower—but he was visibly upset with me as I drove off laughing. *That's what you get for skipping church on the Lord's Day!* What I did was so wrong, but man, did it feel good. (For the record, I've never done it again, and I have since repented of my misdeed.)

But what's the point?

Why didn't that guy hit the ball? Because he was distracted. And I caused it!

I understand that's horrible, but what a great object lesson it is. If he ever gets a copy of this book, he will probably say, "No, I wasn't distracted. I was *afraid* of the *maniac* who almost gave me a heart attack—but I'm willing to smash fear in the mouth."

Touché.

When I was a kid, I had an old Schwinn bicycle with an oversized banana seat. I used to like to take it off some sweet jumps. On this particular day, I hit the ramp at full-pedal speed and got some serious air. Unfortunately, I had been so distracted by my preparations for the jump that I didn't notice that my banana seat was loose. As I went airborne, the seat swiveled upward to a vertical position—and then I landed on it.

Yep. Distractions can be deadly. (Or make you wish you had died.)

Another time, I lost focus and rammed into a parked truck with the first vehicle I had ever purchased, a light blue 1984 Ford Taurus that I'd had for only a couple of weeks. The impact ripped off the passenger-side mirror and left a massive dent in the door. And the worst part of the story is that I had purchased only liability insurance. I never did get my car fixed.

I know what you're thinking: *How in the heck do you hit a parked truck?*

I lost focus.

Before Annette and I had kids, we had an opportunity to knock an item off our adventure list by spending eight days in Hawaii. We took advantage of an all-day excursion that included snorkeling, boogie boarding, and hiking. At our first stop, we spent a couple of hours snorkeling around a coral reef by a breathtaking beach.

When we threw on our fins and masks and dove in, Annette at first had a little trouble breathing through the snorkel. She kept putting her face in the water and then yanking it out.

Come on! Let's go!

Finally, she got the breathing part down, but she was afraid she was going to cut her legs on the coral, so she went out a little farther where the water was deeper. As she began following schools of fish and having fun, she swam farther and farther from the shore.

Uh-oh. She was heading too far out, and I couldn't stop her. She looked like a windup bathtub toy! I started yelling her name, but she kept going. Eventually, she popped her head out of the water and realized she was practically in Japan.

"Get back here!" I yelled. "Hurry!" Annette had been so distracted by the fish that she'd lost focus on where she was and almost got swept out to sea.

Peter allowed the winds and the waves to distract him by moving his eyes from Jesus to the storm. His lack of focus turned him into a short-term water walker. I want to be a long-term water walker.

David says in the Psalms, "I will praise the LORD at all times. I will constantly speak his praises."[13] If we praise the Lord at all times, it's going to be easier to keep our eyes on Jesus.

A great example of someone who demonstrated focus in

action is daredevil Nik Wallenda, who set a world record in 2013 by walking on a tightrope across the Grand Canyon without a safety harness of any kind. Thirteen hundred feet across and 1,500 feet above the canyon floor, it was live television at its finest. Wallenda's feat was so crazy that it began trending on Twitter and almost broke the Internet. It was awesome. It took him 22 minutes and 54 seconds to complete the stunt. Wrap your brain around that one! Almost 23 minutes on a tightrope over the Grand Canyon without a safety net or harness attached to the cable. Did I mention the unpredictable wind gusts? From the safety of my home, I felt as if I were walking with Nik—sweaty palms and all.

What was so amazing—besides the actual stunt—was seeing and hearing Nik Wallenda worship Jesus all the way across the wire. He clearly trusted God. He stepped out onto the cable and made his reckless charge—yes, inch by inch. There was no turning back.

Because he was miked, everyone heard his 23-minute intercession session, which went something like this: "I thank you, Jesus, I'm going to do this. I thank you, God, you're calming the wind. The wind's got to obey. I have authority over the wind."

He was literally speaking to his storm on national television. And he just kept talking to Jesus. In fact, he spoke the name of Jesus more often during his 23 minutes over the canyon than I have as a pastor in the past 17 years—at least it felt like that while I was watching him.

Nik Wallenda embraced his cause. He most definitely smashed fear in the mouth. He clearly shook off the doubters.

He was obviously well prepared. He spoke the Word with authority. He completed his reckless charge by displaying impeccable focus—and set a world record in the process. Love him or hate him, Nik Wallenda is a winner.

Let's be winners!

I will praise the LORD at *all* times.
    I will *constantly* speak his praises.
I will boast only in the LORD;
    let all who are *helpless* take heart.
Come, let us *tell* of the LORD's greatness;
    let us exalt his name together.

I prayed to the LORD, and he *answered* me.
    He *freed* me from all my fears.
Those who *look to him* for help will be radiant with joy;
    no shadow of shame will darken their faces.
In my *desperation* I prayed, and the LORD listened;
    he *saved me* from all my troubles.
For the angel of the LORD is a guard;
    he *surrounds* and defends all who fear him.

Taste and see that the LORD is *good*.
    Oh, the joys of those who take refuge in him![14]

GOD HAS THE LAST WORD

Arlie and Judy Neaville have six kids, 17 grandchildren, and seven or eight great-grandchildren. (I guess when you have that many offspring, they are hard to keep track of.) One thing is for sure: Arlie and Judy don't have a difficult time remembering who has the last word.

I was able to spend 67 minutes on the phone last week with Arlie, a godly, 78-year-old man who has been writing songs and playing music for 61 years. In fact, each year on September 11, his popular song "Pray America" can be heard around the clock on several Southern gospel radio stations. The purpose of my phone call was to hear his son Anthony's story so that I could share it with you.

An amazing couple who attend my church—Jim and Beckie Poole—told me about Arlie and Anthony. Jim is a retired minister of a church where Arlie had been a musical guest several times, so when Jim first told me what had happened to the Neavilles' son, I asked for an opportunity to talk with Arlie.

On June 13, 2013, Arlie and Judy Neaville's adult son—Anthony Wayne Neaville—had an unexpected seizure, passed out, and stopped breathing. He was revived and seemed to bounce back okay, but then he passed out again later that day while on an errand. Upon arrival at the hospital, he was unresponsive, and the doctors put him on life support.

There was no explanation for the incident. Right up until the moment when he collapsed, Anthony had never been seriously ill. He was the father of two sons, a gifted musician, and an athlete who had won multiple awards in high school. What was happening now didn't make any sense.

Tragedy usually doesn't.

Ten days later, the doctors told Arlie and Judy that their otherwise healthy 36-year-old son was brain-dead and had no chance of recovery. Their professional advice to the Neavilles was to pull the plug.

"God's still got the last word," Arlie replied.

Arlie and Judy decided to have the song "Jesus Loves You" played for Anthony 24 hours a day in the hospital. "Jesus Loves You"—not to be confused with the Sunday school standard "Jesus Loves Me"—was written by Arlie and produced by Anthony. Arlie had recorded it at the famous Gaither Studios in Alexandria, Indiana. Perhaps the familiarity of the song and his father's voice would spark some hope for Anthony.

Fifteen days after Arlie and Judy started playing "Jesus Loves You" around the clock for Anthony, the doctors told them point-blank, "Your son is never going to wake up. He is unresponsive. You need to give up."

Arlie's response was the same: "God's still got the last word."

Because his parents refused to pull the plug, Anthony was transferred to a nursing home to live out the rest of his life, however long that might be.

On day 39, Jim Poole, my retired pastor friend, gave a prophetic word to Arlie: "God's going to say, 'Wake up, Sleeping Beauty,' and Anthony is going to wake up."

Pastor Poole's prophetic words came true the very next day. While a nurse was checking his vital signs, Anthony opened his eyes. The nurse went running down the hallway, found Arlie and Judy, and yelled, "Anthony is not brain-dead! He just looked at me!"

In an instant, God flipped the switch from impossible to

possible, from hope deferred to longing fulfilled, from darkness to light, from death to life! This is the kind of story that miracles are made of.

As I spoke with Arlie on the phone about this epic act of God, there was a long pause. When he continued, I couldn't tell if he was crying or laughing, but he said, "Day number 40 ended at 3:00 p.m., and Anthony opened his eyes that evening—which means it was the beginning of day 41!"

> **In an instant, God flipped the switch from impossible to possible, from hope deferred to longing fulfilled, from darkness to light, from death to life!**

Now *I* wasn't sure if I was crying or laughing.

The story doesn't end there. Anthony began a new journey on day 41, a journey that still continues.

On day 70, he turned his head. He was eventually moved to his parents' home to begin home health care and has now been there for more than a year. Anthony can't walk or talk, and he still has breathing and feeding tubes; but he knows who his parents are, and he responds to commands. He is gradually becoming more aware—he even hums songs and has begun making tiny movements. He receives regular speech, occupational, and physical therapy, and the doctors use Botox injections to offset the effects of stronger muscles and allow his brain to regain control of weaker muscles. His doctors are even using Anthony as a case study. His progress proves that he is very much alive . . . and very much a miracle.

Arlie told me—no, Arlie *preached* to me: "The journey

is to become like Christ. He doesn't always take away the troubles, but he promises to be with us."

#StandingOnThePromises
#41WillCome
#RecklessCharge
#Attack

WE WIN!

*So David triumphed over the Philistine with only
a sling and a stone, for he had no sword.*

1 SAMUEL 17:50, NLT

Try + umph = Triumph.

RICK WARREN

AFTER 40 DAYS of soapbox speeches by Goliath and no
response from the other side, one thing was abundantly clear:
Israel had given up.

They had quit.

They were done.

Wasn't nobody ever going out to challenge that giant.

But wait just a minute.

As day 41 dawned, a new player entered the field. A player
who had not quit. A player who would not quit.

There he was, all five-foot-whatever and 17 years old,
with a slingshot, five smooth stones, and the God of the
universe backing him up.

When the dust finally settled in the valley of Elah, something else had become crystal clear. *David had won.*

What about you? Are you inclined to quit? Have you had enough? Is it just too difficult?

Don't get me wrong. I'm not in any way trying to minimize the seriousness of your situation. I'm not saying that your giant isn't big. But I am saying that God is bigger. And he has your back.

If you're one of those people who starts a book by reading the last chapter first, welcome to a new day. You already know how this turns out.

We win!

Have you read to the end of your Bible?

Spoiler alert: We win!

With God in our corner and calling the shots, we are on the road to victory . . . *if we don't quit.*

This book has taken us on a long journey, but we're still standing. It's not about how we feel. It's about faith in what the Word of God says. It's about faith in who God is.

> The fears of the wicked will be fulfilled;
>   the hopes of the godly will be granted.
> When the storms of life come, the wicked are whirled
>   away,
>   but the godly have a lasting foundation.[1]

Now that's something we can *build* on.

I have shared seven keys to keep you holding on when life gets tough. Seven keys to keep you standing strong until a new day dawns. Not on your own—God is holding you up. He is your source and your strength. Don't waver. Don't faint. Don't quit. A breakthrough is around the corner. "If you faint in the day of adversity, your strength is small."[2] That's not you. You are a winner. You know who your enemy is, and you are aware of his schemes.

You have embraced your cause.

You have smashed fear in the mouth.

You have shaken off words of doubt and have knocked down negativity.

You have prepared yourself to fight.

You have fueled up on the Word.

You have attacked!

As my friend and fellow RockChurch pastor Chris Papazis always reminds me, "It's time to be tenacious!" Then after we share a few high fives and fist bumps, he finishes with, "I'm about to have a fit!"

No more hanging your head. No more cursing yourself with your own words. No more allowing your emotions to control you. Let the revelation of God's Word penetrate your heart and permeate your soul. Show some tenacity.

In the movie *Home Alone*, Kate McCallister ends up on a mission to get home to her son. She displays some tenacity when she addresses the airline ticket agent: "This is Christmas, the season of perpetual hope. And I don't care if I have to get out on your runway and hitchhike. If it costs me everything I own, if I have to sell my soul to the devil himself, I am going to get home to my son."

What a great example of perseverance and determination, minus the "sell my soul to the devil" part. If we will attack our giants with that kind of tenacity mixed with faith, we won't lose!

Paul said, "Rejoice in the Lord always."[3] Not some of the time. Not only on the mountaintops. Rejoice in the valleys as well. Rejoice on the battlefield. Rejoice in the storm. Rejoice in the wilderness. Rejoice in the desert. Rejoice when all you can do is stand. Rejoice by faith that you . . . will . . . win!

Forty-one will come. Shout it on day 1, in year 40, and on every day in between.

I have shared a number of stories here in which the number 41 played a decisive role, but the reality is that *41 Will Come* is also metaphorical. It doesn't have to be exactly 41 days or 41 years. (In fact, God, we're ready for a breakthrough *anytime*.)

This book is intended as an encouragement to you to carry on and push ahead. And it's also an example of what can happen when you do.

The publication of *41 Will Come* didn't happen by accident or happenstance. Instead, it's the fulfillment of a dream hatched more than 15 years ago. The journey has been filled with divine appointments, God moments, and glimpses of his supernatural favor . . . but I had to *work*, as well. I knew that God would do his part if I was willing to do mine, but first I had to put my dream and my faith into action. I had to move from *dreaming* to *doing*. As

> Rejoice by faith that you . . . will . . . win! Forty-one will come. Shout it on day 1, in year 40, and on every day in between.

I began to commit my actions (not just my dreams) to God, he began setting my dreams into motion. And before I knew it, I had a life verse: "Commit your actions to the LORD, and your plans will succeed."[4]

I'm an ordinary person who was willing to dream big and work hard—and because of it, you're reading these words. In case you might find it helpful on your own *41 Will Come* journey, let me tell you the story of how I went from merely desiring to write a book to being a published author.

GODWINKS

In 1995, I purchased a new Harvest praise-and-worship album on cassette tape—an album called *41 Will Come*. The title track inspired me to write a sermon with the same name and preach it to my youth group at the time. I had no idea then that my little youth-group sermon would grow into a book 20 years later.

Then in 1999, when I was chaplain of the Peoria Pirates indoor football team, I preached my "41 Will Come" message before the big semifinal playoff game—a game, you'll recall, that we won 41–40. What's so bizarre to me about that outcome is that the final score didn't fully register in my mind until I was on my way home with my friend Mike. As we were driving, he said quietly, "Man, I can't believe the score."

I was like, "Yeah, 41–40."

I almost drove off the road at that point. And that, my friend, was the very moment when my sermon became a book idea.

Looking back, it's still somewhat humorous to me that

I was a team chaplain for seven seasons in a sport that I had never played at any level—well, unless you count college intramurals and backyard glory days. (One of those backyard glory days ended when I broke my hand on Thanksgiving Day, even though there were only three of us playing.)

Before the inaugural indoor season, I had read an article in our local newspaper that Peoria was acquiring a professional arena-football franchise. While reading the article, I felt a light nudge inside that said, *This is an opportunity to encourage and speak into the lives of a group of guys who have big dreams of playing at the next level.*

Okay, it wasn't a little nudge. It was more like a kick in the rear end. Have you ever had an idea hit you so hard that you just knew you had to step out and pursue it immediately? If your answer is yes and you haven't acted on it yet, go do it! Jump! That's exactly how it happened with me. It was an inward prodding that I couldn't ignore. I recognized it as a nudge from the Holy Spirit, and I knew I had to get out of the boat and go for it.

I picked up the phone and called the team's front office.

"Hello, my name is Chuck Tate, and I'm a local pastor. Does your organization have a team chaplain? If not, I'm interested in volunteering."

That short phone call led to a meeting with Peoria Pirates head coach, Bruce Cowdrey.

Let me tell you a little bit about Bruce Cowdrey. On the field, he's a large, intimidating character, who entertains and works the crowd with his animated antics. He's a loud, no-nonsense, tell-it-like-it-is, passionate firecracker, and he doesn't put up with guff from anyone, including referees. Off the field, he's a very kind and soft-spoken teddy bear.

Cowdrey became a legend in Peoria by winning an Indoor Football League Gold Cup in 2002, with a perfect 17–0 season, and he was also the winningest playoff coach in af2, which was the arena football development league.[5] He later accepted a job coaching the special teams for the Chicago Rush of the Arena Football League, and the team won a nationally televised championship in 2006.

I still remember driving to the practice facility with nervous anticipation. I prayed for peace, favor, and God's will to trump anything else. I had butterflies in my stomach as I walked in and approached the Goliath-like coach. (Did I mention that he can be intimidating?)

Before I could even get a word out, he locked eyes with me and said, "Are you that guy who wants to be our chaplain?"

I was almost afraid to answer, but of course I said, "Yes, sir."

"You're it."

I was somewhat surprised that, within a matter of seconds and without knowing anything about me, he had already accepted my offer. Still taken aback, I hesitantly said, "Uh, I brought you a packet of information about me and our church, since—"

"I don't need that," he growled. "You're the new padre."

Still kind of shocked, I said, "Okay."

"There are just a couple things you need to know, though, son. One, chapel is not mandatory. We're not going to cram it down anyone's throat. And two, I cuss like a sailor—" he paused and fixed me with a piercing stare "—but I love the good Lord."

Without the Holy Spirit's nudge and my obedience to step outside my comfort zone to do something I had never done before, this book wouldn't exist. Not only did my chapel message and the final score of that playoff game inspire this book, but it floored every player who attended that chapel. It also affected players every season after that, as I used the story as a testimony to kick off each new season.

In November 2010, I spoke by phone with author and consultant Jim Kochenburger to get some counsel and feedback about my writing aspirations. After I sent him potential chapter titles and summaries, his encouragement and wisdom steered me in the right direction.

Then there was the time when my mother-in-law called me, excited about an advertisement for a writing contest she had clipped from *Reader's Digest*. At the time, I was still pretty unfamiliar with book proposals, and I didn't have enough time to enter the contest, but that moment inspired me to begin working on my craft. It also gave me hope.

Have you ever heard somebody say something that you just knew was for you? One time when I was watching the Seeds Conference live via satellite from Church on the Move in Tulsa, pastor Shannon O'Dell said, "Somebody out there has a book inside of him." That hit me just right, and I took that one as *mine*.

Along the way, I sat in a Steak 'n Shake at two in the morning with my close friend Dave Mudd, dreaming about the possibilities of writing and publishing this book. Dave reached across the table and handed me an inspirational bracelet he'd gotten from the Magic Johnson Foundation. It's a black, woven cord with a little metal tab attached that has the word PREVENT on one side and the word EMPOWER on the other.

"*Prevent* means everything that's stopping you from writing the book," he said, "and *empower* represents that you are already empowered by God to write it. So every time you look at it, I want you to hear me saying, 'Write the dang book, Chuck!'"

So, yeah, even my friends were tired of hearing me talk about it. And the thing is, it worked! Every day, I could hear Dave's voice in my head, shouting, "Write the dang book!"

At one point, I turned my *41 Will Come* book idea into an eight-week sermon series at RockChurch. I had all eight sermons transcribed by my friend Debbie Seaborn, and just like that I had some serious content to pull from.

Then there was the time when a woman in our congregation was so inspired by the "41 Will Come" series that she had *41 Will Come* tattooed on her wrist. That's investing in hope!

One day, my friend Cecil called me and said, "Hey, Chuck, on my flight yesterday, I sat next to one of the Dallas Cowboys players." Cecil knows I'm a huge Cowboys fan. Then he added, "I told him all about your book idea and the Peoria Pirates story. He was very interested in it and loved the concept." (#BoomGoesTheDynamite)

In October 2013, my friend and mentor Jim Powell (author of *Dirt Matters*) invited me to a writers conference called Re:Write because he believed in my concept. The only problem was that the conference was scheduled for the same day as my 17th wedding anniversary. I'll be honest: I was nervous even bringing it up with my wife. Up to that point, I had never missed an anniversary, and we had never been apart on that day. I was relieved and overjoyed when she said, "This is a huge opportunity. You have to go!" I went, truly believing that God would use that conference for preparation, training, and networking.

Little did I realize.

At that conference, bestselling author Mark Batterson kicked me in the face—okay, he didn't actually kick me in the face, but what he said motivated me to action. During his keynote address, he asked us all something like this: "How many here tonight feel called by God to write? Some write because it's therapeutic or a hobby. Some of you just enjoy writing. I want to know how many of you feel *called* by God to write?"

Hands went up all over the conference room—including mine.

Now for the kick in the face: "You are living in disobedience if you are not writing."

Repentance followed. I began writing again.

At that same conference, I approached (with wobbly knees) the inimitable Esther Fedorkevich to request one minute of her time to share my book concept and (I hoped) receive an honest assessment and any constructive input she had to offer.

(By the way, I almost chickened out. When it comes to

the world of literary agents, Esther's a rock star. I had to shake off my doubt and smash fear in the mouth. I personally equate this moment to when Peter jumped out of the boat. I will never forget how, when I asked her for a minute, she answered point blank: "Go!")

This was my "rawk stance" moment. I had already practiced and rehearsed what I was going to say, so my preparation gave me the confidence to plow through with my pitch.

Her response after my spiel pleasantly surprised me: "I love the idea, but I don't know if you can write. Do you have a proposal?"

Uh.

"Finish your book proposal, write a big *41* on it, and I won't forget it."

Uh, okay. Thanks!

As I walked away, tears welled up in my eyes. This was the validation and encouragement I needed to keep going.

During the summer of 2014, I was scrolling through my Twitter feed and found a notice for something called Book Proposal Academy, put on by creativity coach Chad Allen (who had been another one of the featured speakers at the 2013 Re:Write Conference and was also an acquisitions editor for Baker Books). I enrolled right at the deadline. Little did I know that his 10-week course would educate, instruct, inspire, and inject confidence in me to follow through with writing my proposal.

That and every time I looked down at my bracelet, I heard my friend Dave's voice say, "Write the dang book!"

When I finally had a completed proposal, I requested

prayer from my congregation at RockChurch because I was about to enter it into a national writing contest to take a crack at winning a book deal (so I could finally publish the book they had been hearing about and waiting on for a really long time). I almost backed out of entering, but because I had already announced it from the stage, I felt obligated to keep my word.

Thank God for accountability.

In December 2014, my family and I traveled with some close friends to Wisconsin Dells for a five-day getaway—right on the deadline for the writing contest. My wife drove. I typed. When we arrived at our cabin, I hammered away on my laptop like an overage kid on the Whack-A-Mole at Chuck E. Cheese.

The kids played in the other room.

I typed.

The wives went grocery shopping for the week.

I typed.

The ladies returned and unloaded the food.

I typed.

The kids went to bed.

I typed.

Annette watched me from a distance.

I typed.

As the midnight deadline approached, I was unhappy with my manuscript.

Too bad.

It was now 11:59 p.m. Time was up.

Uh-oh. I didn't have the e-mail address.

"No!" I screamed, not caring whom I woke up. "God, I need another hour!"

I frantically searched the website for the e-mail address, all the while realizing that my proposal would be time-stamped late and I was about to miss the cut.

Wait a minute.

While scanning for the e-mail address, I noticed that the website said proposals had be submitted by 12:00 a.m. *Pacific Time.* I was in the Central Time Zone. I had not one but *two* more hours.

Hallelujah! I'm pretty sure I heard angels singing . . . or God laughing. Again, I was overwhelmed by God's grace and mercy.

One hour and 55 minutes later, I hit "send" and submitted my official book proposal for the Re:Write writing contest. Five minutes to spare. (Sigh of relief.)

On January 1, 2015, I started checking the Re:Write Conference website every 12 seconds to see if I had made the Top 10. Finally a notice was posted that the official announcement would be delayed because of so many great submissions.

Uh-oh.

The contest sponsor, Tyndale House Publishers, needed more time to deliberate.

Ugh. This is killing me!

I will never forget the moment when I received a Twitter notification from @ReWriteConf that the votes were in. I clicked on the app and scrolled through the post looking for one familiar name—and there it was!

Chuck Tate.

With tears welling up, I praised God without reservation and called my wife to share the good news. When I got home that day, my kids went crazy. (#HappyDance)

THAT TIME I WON A BOOK DEAL

Fast-forward to February 27, 2015. I'm sitting in a packed meeting room in Austin, Texas—a room filled with aspiring writers, published authors, industry executives, and other assorted world changers, as they are about to name the winner of the contest.

A flood of emotions engulfed me when I heard them announce, "The winner of the 2015 Tyndale Momentum/Re:Write and The Ragged Edge Writing Contest is . . . Chuck Tate."

After a long pause, I stood up.

Did she really just call my name?

My knees buckled.

Cheers.

Applause.

My friend Jason, who was with me and sitting next to me, was flat-out losing his mind! I have the video footage he shot on his phone to prove it.

As I approached the stage, I felt as if I were wading through a swimming pool—a swimming pool filled with peanut butter.

Twenty minutes later (not really, but it sure felt like it), I found myself on stage, receiving a plaque and shaking hands with Jan Long Harris of Tyndale House

Publishers and literary agent Esther Fedorkevich of the Fedd Agency.

The plaque I clutched in my hands was much more than just a shiny decoration or a cool piece of art for my office wall. I had just won a major publishing contract to publish the book you are holding in your hands. I would not have to pursue Plan B—which was to create a Kickstarter campaign to self-publish my concept. The plaque confirmed that I would publish *41 Will Come* with Tyndale Momentum and that I would be represented by Esther Fedorkevich.

In case you're thinking, *Dude, you won a book deal, not the Nobel Prize. No need to get all crazy on me,* let me tell you how, for me, this was so much more than a book deal. It was God's stamp of approval on an idea he had deposited in my heart more than 15 years earlier. For the previous 5,475 days, I had talked about it, preached it, prayed over it, and dreamed about it—without actually writing it. Why? There are countless reasons, but they are mainly busyness, procrastination, fear, excuses, and the rigors of life, to name just a few. There were so many nights through all those years when I would lie in bed and wonder whether it would ever come to fruition.

When will I have time?

When will I make time?

Will my dream-come-true have someone else's fingerprints on it?

Will my book idea have someone else's name on it?

I thank God for his grace because I made oodles of mistakes along the way, and there are several things I would do differently or do over completely. But looking back, one thing is crystal clear: God's fingerprints are evident throughout my journey. My far-reaching adventure has been filled with divine appointments, decisive moments, crucial events, and coincidental encounters that can be explained only by what my friend and fellow author Julie Lyles Carr calls a Godwink.

YEA, THOUGH I WALK THROUGH THE VALLEY OF FEVER . . .

Coccidioidomycosis. I'm not sure how to pronounce it, but I can tell you it's too long of a word to use in Scrabble and that it's a disease—one that almost killed me when I was a kid. The fungus that causes *coccidioidomycosis* lives in the soil and dust of the southwestern United States, which includes my boyhood hometown of Phoenix, Arizona. The abbreviated name is *cocci*, but the common name is "valley fever." According to the Mayo Clinic, valley fever is a fungal infection that can cause fever, chest pain, and coughing, along with other symptoms. I can tell you that it's no fun, especially for a five-year-old.

Unfortunately, I had a severe case. My dad remembers being told by my doctor that only five cases in 1,000 are fatal—but they believed I might be one of the five because they thought the infection had spread throughout my body.

How's that for cheerful news?

My mom was amazed that, on the very night I was admitted to Maricopa County Hospital, I looked up at her from my bed and said, "Mommy, you look tired. Go home and get some rest and see me in the morning."

I had no idea how sick I was.

Because there was a chance that I had tuberculosis instead of valley fever, and because I had developed pneumonia, I spent the first ten days in isolation. The doctors were actually hoping it was TB because the treatment for valley fever was almost as bad as the disease itself.

Not long after the diagnosis was confirmed, my mom overheard a group of doctors in the hallway talking about the sad fate of some little boy.

(For your information, my mom has bionic ears. Not really, but really. Seriously, I don't know where you are reading this right now, but if you will start reading aloud, I'm pretty sure my mom will hear you. Yes, this is ironic considering that I am hearing impaired. But it is nonetheless true. So it wasn't that the doctors were talking too loud.)

Alarmed by what she had heard, my mom confronted the doctors, and they acknowledged that they had been talking about me. The news was almost too much to bear.

Back in the 1970s, parents weren't permitted to spend the night in the rooms with patients. Besides that, I had a one-year-old brother at home. Dad and Mom took turns watching Denny so that the other could be with me at the hospital. One night, Mom came in to say good night before going home to sleep. When she came into the room, I gave her a picture I had drawn of Jesus on the cross. I preached to her that night about the price Jesus had paid, and I explained the gospel in great detail.

Mom went home crying that night, perhaps wondering whether God was preparing me to meet Jesus. When she arrived at our house, she told my dad what had happened.

"I think the Lord is getting ready to take Chuckie," she said through tears.

My dad was overcome with emotion, but after a moment he responded quietly, "He can have him."

"No! You don't understand!" my mom screamed. "You didn't give birth to him!"

It was an emotional moment to say the least, and afterward my parents went into separate rooms to pray. During Dad's prayer time, God assured him that I was going to live.

The next day, Mom received a phone call that I was going to be moved into the ICU and that they were going to begin IV treatment. My future looked bleak, but Mom told God emphatically, "Please don't take my son! Please don't take my son!"

In her spirit, she sensed God's response: *Why not? I gave you my only Son. You have two.*

Ouch! When my mom first told me this story, her account of God's response seemed so abrupt and almost harsh. But Mom has a robust faith, and she says that God knew what was needed to get her attention and draw her toward a deeper trust in him.

Broken and bereft by God's severe mercy, my mom finally surrendered her will. "Okay. You can have him."

This part of the story reminds me that God, in his wisdom, always speaks into the depths of our need—even when it might hurt. Another example that comes to mind is the amazing experience that our student pastor, Cory Vance, and his wife, Sarah, had when their daughter, Moriah, was born.

Sarah, is a type 1 diabetic, and because of that and other

health concerns, she was told by multiple doctors that she could never have children.

But God had a better plan. Sarah became pregnant and delivered a beautiful baby girl. However, some complications during the delivery caused little Moriah's heart to stop beating. She was dead for almost a minute.

During those 50 seconds, Cory prayed, "God, you didn't bring Moriah miraculously into this world only to have her die upon arrival . . . but if it's your will, I'm okay with that."

In his spirit, he heard God respond, *Don't be afraid. Just believe.*

When Cory told this story a few weeks ago during a sermon, there wasn't a dry eye in the room.

As you may have guessed, Moriah pulled through. Not only were the doctors able to shock her heart back to life, but she seemed not to have suffered any ill effects from the time when she was clinically dead. Today, she's almost two years old and can occasionally be seen dancing in our sanctuary during worship. And she's slightly afraid of me.

Back to my own story. My future did not look promising as my illness continued. Eleven specialists from California were working on my case because it was uncommon for a young, Caucasian child to be so severely affected. I was losing weight and getting weaker; but my parents refused to lose hope, and they continued to stand on the Word of God.

As a last resort, the doctors placed me on a highly toxic IV therapy that can cause kidney damage. Right around that time, God used a sermon about Jehovah Rapha—the God who heals—to give Mom a quiet confidence that the Lord was with me and would see me through.

He spoke to her, saying, "I am the Lord your God. I will give Chuckie the treatment, and everything will be okay."

While God was moving in Mom's heart, to all appearances it seemed pretty imminent that I was about to become a statistic—one of the five-in-a-thousand fatal cases of valley fever.

Because this was in the dark and distant past before we had social media, the only way to get people praying was for church members to call everyone on their list of prayer warriors—something the old-school churches call "the prayer chain." Today, prayer chains consist of Facebook threads and viral tweets. But back then it was people calling people and then getting on their knees. The bottom line is that people began to pray. Our church was praying. My pastor, Don Grosvenor, came into the hospital to pray for me. The prayer chain was in motion, and God was working behind the scenes.

> **Wearing the armor of God protects us. Prayer, the sword of the Spirit, and the power of God win battles.**

And then there was the Dad factor.

After getting prayed up at home, my dad showed up at the hospital in a reckless charge, ready to fight the enemy. He had had enough. It was time to put his foot down—on the devil's neck. Defense might win championships in sports, but in life we have to go on the offensive to kill giants. Wearing the armor of God protects us. Prayer, the sword of the Spirit (which is God's Word), and the power of God win battles.

My parents put on the required protective hospital garb and strutted into my isolation room full of audacious faith and a little bit of swagger. Before they prayed, my mom asked me, "Are you going to heaven with Mommy and Daddy or are you going a different time?"

"I'm going with you guys," Mom later told me I replied. "And when we go"—I lifted both of my arms upward—"the sky will be full of people because the Spirit of Jesus is going to lift us all to heaven."

Dad took off one of his latex gloves, slapped his hand onto my chest, and prayed as if my life depended on it—because it did. He took authority over the spirit of valley fever, and of death, and began to speak the Word of Life over my body.

Later, as my parents walked out of my room, Dad looked at Mom and said confidently, "Chuckie will be in a regular room tomorrow."

Word up.

Speak to your storm.

Bring the boom.

When my parents showed up the next day, I wasn't in isolation. I wasn't in the ICU. I had been moved into a regular room. (*Boom* goes the dynamite!) And not only had I been moved into a regular room, but I also had a roommate.

Actually, Johnny was more than a roommate. He became my new fishing partner. Remember, this was 1975, when the times and the technology were so much different from today's. There was no Xbox or PlayStation, no Minecraft, no Blu-ray players, cell phones, or game controllers. Instead, I passed the time by moving my electronic bed up and down while pretending to be on a boat. Johnny and I used my toy fishing poles to pretend we were deep-sea fishing.

Even though my parents were grateful when I was released from isolation, they weren't done praying for the mountain to move. During the entire three weeks I had been in the hospital, I'd had a high fever every day. So Dad continued his spiritual stampede by declaring, "Chuckie's not going to have a fever today."

Not long after he said this, a nurse came into the room for a routine vitals check. She took my temperature, and the thermometer registered normal.

Hmm. That's strange. It was clear from the expression on her face that she thought the thermometer had malfunctioned. After slapping it a couple of times, she took my temperature again.

Normal.

This can't be right.

She left the room to retrieve a new thermometer and then took my temperature one last time.

Normal—98.6.

I went home three days later.

I was released on a Sunday, and my parents took me straight to church. Go figure. Story of my life.

I continued outpatient IV therapy every other day for four months before the doctors made me stop for fear of kidney damage.

Fast-forward to the present day: My kidneys are just fine.

By the way, my healing took place exactly 40 years ago.

Forty-one really has come for me. And I believe your 41

is on its way. In the words of T. D. Jakes, "Get ready. Get ready. Get ready. Get ready!"

Thank you for going on this journey with me. I am immensely humbled that you picked up this book and read it to the end. I hope you dreamed, laughed, and cried along with me. And if you're the only one, it was still worth it. This book may include stories from my journey, but I wrote it to help you with yours.

Dream.

Do.

Repeat.

#41WillCome
#PrayingThrough

WHEN 41 DOESN'T COME

Why am I discouraged? Why is my heart so sad? I will put my hope in God! I will praise him again—my Savior and my God!

PSALM 42:11, NLT

"WE LOST HER, BROTHER."

I will never forget the demoralizing text message I received one Saturday afternoon in October 2014. My heart sank as my mind went numb with disbelief. I had just finished performing a wedding and was about to blow bubbles at the bride. Instead, my own faith bubble burst, and I felt as if I were about to crumble. I exited the wedding celebration, climbed into my car, and called my new friend and fellow parishioner, Dan. His 16-year-old daughter, Lindsey, had just slipped into eternity.

Two polar-opposite life events collided that day: one happy, one sad; one new beginning, one sad ending; one congratulatory hug, one condolence-filled phone call.

Life is filled with ups and downs; mountains and valleys; faith and doubt; moments when fresh wind fills our spiritual sails and moments when we lose our breath after being punched in the gut by unforeseen circumstances. Sometimes 41 doesn't come. Sometimes 41 passes us by. Sometimes 41 is the day or the year of the funeral. So it seems.

LINDSEY'S STORY

The previous Sunday, October 12, was a routine Sunday morning. It also happened to be my birthday. I stood in the front row of the sanctuary, worshiping as I do every weekend. As our band rocked through the song "Break Every Chain," I felt a strong impression from the Holy Spirit that someone in the room was suicidal.

I ignored the tug. Worship continued.

The Holy Spirit prodded me again—more strongly this time, but still I questioned whether I was indeed hearing from God.

As the worship song moved into its final stanza, I knew that if I were going to make a move, it would have to be then. Once the song ended, Lance, our worship pastor, would initiate a minute-long "meet and greet" time for the congregation, and the moment would be lost.

I decided I would rather interrupt the program and be wrong than to be right and disobedient. I quickly stepped up onto the stage and slid over next to Lance as he ended the song.

"This doesn't happen very often," I said to the congregation, "but I feel very strongly that someone in this room contemplated taking their own life last night. God is using me to stop this service to get your attention and reveal to you how significant you are, how much you matter, and how much he loves you. If I'm talking to *you*, I want you to come to the stage right now. I'm going to pray for you, and I believe God is going to heal your heart and heal your hurt."

I was surprised when several people responded. The first person was a middle-aged woman named Dolly Gleason who practically tackled me when she collapsed into my arms and sobbed like a baby as God rescued her. She went home after the service and penned the following words:

> *Tears that you don't see . . .*
> *The pain you don't feel . . .*
> *The tears that fall inside . . .*
> *Tears of seeing both sides . . .*
> *Heart, mind, body, soul . . .*
> *Tears of release from all!*[1]

Another person who responded was a 16-year-old girl named Lindsey. Tears flowed. Prayers were offered. The worship time was extended. Healing was in the house. Then everyone who had responded went quietly back to their seats, and we continued with the service.

I wasn't prepared for what would happen five days later.

The following Friday evening, Lindsey's father, Dan, asked me to call him. His message explained that he and Lindsey's stepmother, Cherity, were at their wits' end with their troubled teenage daughter.

A few minutes into our conversation, he interrupted me. "Hold on a second."

A loud commotion in the background soon followed.

"What did you do?" I heard Dan say with alarm in his voice.

I couldn't decipher everything, but I heard enough to know it wasn't good.

"I'm going to have to call you back, Pastor Chuck. Please pray."

I prayed and anxiously awaited his call.

A few minutes later, Dan called me back from his car and explained that they were on their way to the emergency room because Lindsey had swallowed 300 aspirin. We prayed together over the phone, and after we hung up, I ran upstairs to tell Annette. We prayed together. And then we waited.

Dan had called around 10:00 p.m., so as the night wore on, all we could do was hope that no news was good news.

While waiting to hear whether I should meet the family at the hospital, I received a text message from a friend in Dallas who was pitching a television show about missions to some major secular networks. She asked whether Annette and I wanted to watch a short video sampler of the show. She sent us a link, and we decided to gather the kids so we could all experience it together.

The 10-minute sizzle reel featured an organization called the World Race, which launches twentysomethings on an intense missions assignment that includes visiting 11 countries in 11 months.[2] I was floored by the passion for the gospel that oozed from every frame. One quotation that burned into my skull went something like this: "The Jesus we're seeing in action on the mission field isn't the same Jesus that is being preached about in the pulpits."

Boom!

We shut off the television, and I exclaimed to my wife and kids, "That makes me want to drive to the airport right now, jump on a plane, and fly overseas straight to the mission field!"

Without missing a beat, my wife responded, "Maybe you should start by jumping in your car and driving straight to the hospital."

Ouch! Message received.

I love the Holy Spirit, and I love my wife. Sometimes I can't tell the two apart. Perhaps it's just that my wife is more attentive to the Holy Spirit's prodding than I am. Regardless, she was right. It had been a long night that included a wedding rehearsal and rehearsal dinner, and by now it was close to midnight; but I knew what I needed to do.

One reason why I had been waiting to hear, rather than driving straight to the hospital, was that Dan and Cherity were somewhat new to the church, and I didn't want to impose myself on them because I didn't know them very well at the time. Some people are private about their struggles. Others assume you have seen their Facebook posts and expect you to be there even in a blizzard. Ahh, the life of a pastor.

During the 25-minute drive to the hospital, I blared worship songs in the car and prayed. When I arrived, a nurse escorted me into the emergency room, where Lindsey and her family were, including her mom, Linda. Apart from the immediate side effect of hyperventilating, Lindsey was more than alert and responsive. In fact, she was smiling and even joking around. It was evident that she believed, along with her parents, that she would eventually be released from the hospital, make a full recovery, and be just fine.

As we all gathered around Lindsey's bed, I began sharing encouraging Scripture verses about self-worth, and I expressed to Lindsey how much she mattered to God and how much God loved her. As tears welled up in her eyes, I could sense that she believed me and was truly remorseful for what she had done.

So why did she do it? Why had she taken 300 aspirin in the first place? She was completely broken and tired of being bullied. I asked her whether I could pray for her. She simply nodded and quietly said, "Yes."

I laid my hand on her shoulder and began to pray for physical and emotional healing and for God to reveal to her in a big way how much he truly loved her. It was such an important moment—a moment I would have missed if not for Annette's responsiveness to the Holy Spirit.

By morning, Lindsey had been placed on dialysis, and even though there was still a great amount of concern and suspense, it appeared that she was improving and out of the woods—so much so that Dan left the room to stretch his legs and grab a quick bite in the cafeteria. While sitting in the cafeteria, he received a text message from Linda, Lindsey's mom, to get back to the room ASAP. By the time he reached Lindsey's side, her organs had begun to shut down. The physicians and staff did everything within their power to save her, but sadly, it wasn't enough. Her body just could not overcome the destructive effects of that much aspirin. At 12:06 p.m., Lindsey's time on earth expired.

RUNNING TO THE RESCUER

What do you do when 41 doesn't come? What do you do when the answer you so desperately wanted dissolves right before your eyes? What do you do when your heart is ripped out and you have already shed so many tears that you can't even cry anymore?

Monumental moments like these present two options: blame God or run to him. It may seem easier to shake your fist at God and climb into a hole of hatred and despair.

Easier, maybe, but not better.

When you choose to run away from God, you run away from hope. When you run toward Jesus, you run straight into the arms of the God who rescues, *Jehovah Yesha* (literally, *the Lord is salvation*). He is the only one who can unequivocally sustain you in your suffering.

> When you choose to run away from God, you run away from hope. When you run toward Jesus, you run straight into the arms of the God who rescues.

"The LORD is close to the brokenhearted; he rescues those whose spirits are crushed."[3] This Scripture isn't theoretical. It wasn't written by someone who hadn't experienced loss. It was penned by King David, who knew firsthand what it was like to stomach the excruciating pain of losing a young child, having his father-in-law hate him to the extent of trying to murder him, and being betrayed and hunted down by his own son—the same son who would later die by being hung up in a tree by his own hair.

King David ran to the Rescuer. Will you? Will you hang on and stand strong? You do this by remembering the Word, reading the Word, and anchoring yourself to the Word.

> Don't be afraid, I've redeemed you.
>   I've called your name. You're mine.
> When you're in over your head, I'll be there with you.
>   When you're in rough waters, you will not go down.
> When you're between a rock and a hard place,
>   it won't be a dead end—
> Because I am GOD, your personal God.[4]

Here's a dose of truth: You can remember the Word, read the Word, and anchor yourself to the Word, but you need more than the Word.

Please don't take this the wrong way. Hear me out.

Yes, Jesus is all you need for eternal life, but if you are going to survive this life, you will need to surround yourself with people who will help you hold up your arms of faith.

There's a remarkable—and literal—example of this in Exodus. During Israel's 40-year journey through the wilderness, they were attacked by the Amalekites, so Moses instructed his young protégé, Joshua, to choose some capable men to fight the army of Amalek. Meanwhile, Moses went to the top of a mountain, along with his brother, Aaron, and a trusted companion named Hur. Moses stood there and held up the staff of God in his hand. As long as he raised the staff, the Israelites prevailed on the battlefield. But whenever his arms dropped, the Amalekites gained the advantage.

> Moses' arms soon became so tired he could no longer hold them up. So Aaron and Hur found a stone for him to sit on. Then they stood on each side of Moses, holding up his hands. So his hands held steady until sunset. As a result, Joshua overwhelmed the army of Amalek in battle.
>
> After the victory, the LORD instructed Moses, "Write this down on a scroll as a permanent reminder."[5]

Consider this your reminder. Sometimes the only way to hold on is to be held up. We can't do it alone. We need other people. We need support. We need accountability. We need encouragement. This is why the apostle Paul writes, "If one part [of the body] suffers, every part suffers with it."[6]

Hebrews 10:25 says, "Some people have gotten out of the habit of meeting for worship, but we must not do that. We should keep on encouraging each other, especially since you know that the day of the Lord's coming is getting closer."[7]

This confirms that it is just as important for the church to *be* the church as it is for us to simply attend church. Yes, the Word is important. Yes, worship is important. But we cannot and must not forget the importance of encouraging, comforting, and consoling one another.

KNOW YOUR WORTH

One of the first individuals to reach out to Dan following his daughter's suicide was a friend of mine named Jill. Jill had lost her daughter, Hannah, to suicide only a month before Dan lost Lindsey. Hannah had been a beautiful 18-year-old girl with a world of potential. In fact, just before her death, she told her mom that her next tattoo, inked on her shoulder, would consist of the phrase *Know Your Worth*.

Sadly, Hannah didn't understand her own worth. It was fitting, then, that five of Hannah's closest friends got *Know Your Worth* tattoos in her honor, just in time for her celebration-of-life service. And what do you think I preached about at her funeral? *Worth.*

After the service, Jill took to social media and began a campaign called the Know Your Worth Project, in Hannah's honor. She began reaching out to teenagers who were victims of bullying and depression. She began reaching out to parents of other suicide victims. She used her pain as a platform to help others . . . including Dan. She introduced herself at Lindsey's service and told Dan and his family that they weren't alone. Thank God for people like Jill.

It hasn't been easy, though. There were (and still are) days when Jill has felt like quitting, but those who are close to her won't let her. There were days early on when Dan thought about stepping in front of a semitruck because the lingering sting of Lindsey's death still ripped him to the core and seemed too unbearable to carry. I still have text messages from him that vented his questions, anger, and despair. But we held up his arms, and onward he went.

Dan began spending a lot of time in his woodshop creating plaques in Lindsey's honor to give to parents of suicide victims. He even made one for me with our church logo that is in my office, a logo that I have tattooed on my arm as a reminder of our vision. It's the same kind of reminder for Dan to use Lindsey's death as a means to bring life—to allow God to bring good out of what the devil intended for evil. This is Romans 8:28 in action.

OPERATION ANCHORED

Dan and Cherity have launched a campaign called Operation Anchored: 4 Love, Hope & Worth. Here's what it means:

> *Operation* represents Dan's desire, as a military veteran, to put a dent in the staggering statistic that 24 US veterans attempt suicide each day.
>
> *Anchored* stands for Lindsey's plan, before she died, to get an anchor tattoo with the text *Refuse to Sink*.
>
> *The numeral 4* represents the soccer number of a young man named Connor who took his own life.
>
> *Love* represents a teenage girl named Colby who took her own life. (By the way, her parents now attend our church because of Dan.)
>
> *Hope* stands as a reminder never to lose hope.
>
> *Worth* is in loving memory of Hannah.

In just a few short months, Operation Anchored raised more than $15,000 for suicide prevention.

A few weeks ago, Dan approached me and announced, "I'm ready to share my story." We scheduled him to participate in our "Run to the Roar" sermon series, which is based in part on Levi Lusko's book, *Through the Eyes of a Lion*—a gut-wrenching yet inspirational story of how Pastor Levi learned that the pain of losing his little girl could become a "microphone" for bringing other people to Christ. It is one of the best books on sustaining loss and suffering that I've ever read.

When the day came for Dan to speak, he and I sat onstage for all three weekend services and talked, cried, and prayed together as he vulnerably shared his heart and his hurt with those in attendance. He demonstrated what it means to use pain as a microphone, and people responded. An invitation at the end of each service resulted in a handful of people coming to Christ and numerous others coming to the altar to receive prayer for their sadness and suffering.

Dan stepped off the stage with me to pray with everyone who came forward. Then many others came forward to hold up the arms of those who had responded. Tears. Lots of tears. Some wailing. Joy in the midst of sadness. Healing was in the house. It was a beautiful demonstration of the church being the church.

This was the same weekend during which Dan and Cherity launched a grief support group at our church for parents who have lost a child to suicide. Eight parents attended the first meeting, all eight of them were in church, and all eight—including Hannah's mom, Jill—were at the altar holding one another up.

Regarding his own struggle with depression, Dwayne "The Rock" Johnson said, "Hold on to that fundamental quality of faith. Have faith. . . . And on the other side of your pain is something good."[8]

Pain can become a platform. Good can come from bad. You can choose joy in the midst of extreme sadness. It just requires faith. You must believe it! When 41 doesn't come, you can succumb to defeat, or you can allow God to reveal a new 41 on the other side of your pain. Dan's original 41 was for Lindsey to survive the aspirin poisoning of her system. His new 41 is to prevent as many people as possible from trying to take their own lives. His initial 41 was for his daughter to be healed. His new 41 is to help bring healing to those who have experienced the same type of loss that he encountered.

WHEN GOD DOESN'T ANSWER

Allow me to revisit the end of Isaiah 43:3 from Eugene Peterson's *The Message*: "Because I am God, your personal God."

God is your personal God. When you cry out to him, he hears you. He sees you. He understands you. He gets you. After all, you're his creation, his workmanship.[9] He says, "Call to me and I will answer you."[10] Because I'm a pastor, I hear the following statement all the time: "When I pray, my prayers don't seem to go anywhere. God doesn't answer me." Sound familiar? So what should you do when God doesn't seem to answer? Here are five things.

1. Keep Praying

Daniel was instructed to quit praying or be thrown into a lion's den. If that deadly threat didn't stop him, do you think an unanswered prayer would stop him? No way! He kept talking to God. The devil wants you to stop praying. Don't.

2. Keep Listening

Sometimes God answers, but we aren't paying attention. Don't stop listening. God moments and divine appointments are easy to miss because of busyness or frustration. God also gives countless answers through his Word. We won't find them if we don't take the time to look—and listen.

3. Keep Waiting

Too many people miss out because they quit right before the breakthrough. Don't be one of them. There have been a handful of crucial moments in my life when I was tempted to throw in the towel. If I had, you wouldn't be reading this book because it wouldn't exist. And having read chapter 11, you know how long I had to wait to see this book come to fruition. The prophet Habakkuk says, "This vision is for a future time. It describes the end, and it will be fulfilled. If it seems slow in coming, wait patiently, for it will surely take place. It will not be delayed."[11]

4. Keep Moving

Don't get complacent. Don't put your life on hold while you wait. God is moving behind the scenes. You have to keep putting one foot in front of the other. Carry on. You can only see where you are right now. God sees where he is going to take you. As Goethe once said, "Doubt of any kind can only be removed by action."[12]

5. Keep Remembering

Let your past victories fuel your faith for future victories. Countless times in the Old Testament, God instructs his people to set up some type of memorial after a huge victory so that they wouldn't forget.

> This is what GOD says,
>> the God who builds a road right through the ocean,
>> who carves a path through pounding waves,
> The God who summons horses and chariots and
>> armies—
>> they lie down and then can't get up;
>> they're snuffed out like so many candles.[13]

"Do not despise these small beginnings."[14] Uncover your past. Recount God's greatness in your life. Remember his faithfulness to you. By the indwelling power of the Holy Spirit, you have greatness inside you, and a "poor me" attitude isn't going to help you. Don't forget what God has already done in your life! Every day is a gift.

Amanda Noelle was at our church recently to share about her cancer journey, and she said something that is still bouncing around in my head: "When you feel entitled to something, you won't feel grateful for it."

Each day is a gift. Remember what God has already brought you through.

ISRAEL FORGOT

One would think that if a nation had witnessed God's wrath being poured out on their enemy—not once, but ten times—they wouldn't question him again. But not Israel. Not only did God demonstrate his power by inflicting plague after plague upon Egypt, but he also supernaturally freed Israel following 400 years of bondage. God even granted them favor with the Egyptians so they could plunder Egypt of its wealth on their way out of town. But as soon as they ran into their first obstacle—the Red Sea—they lamented to Moses that it would have been better if they had remained in Egypt as slaves.

Next, God performed one of the most awe-inspiring miracles in the history of the world by ripping the Red Sea apart and paving a way for the people to pass through on dry ground. What a magnificent display of God's power! I can only hope that if I had participated in the Red Sea rendezvous, I would never doubt God again. On the other hand, I *have* witnessed numerous miracles and yet I still find myself forgetting.

More miracles and moaning followed before God eventually summoned Moses for a chat on Mt. Sinai. Interestingly enough, that confab lasted 40 days. While Moses was as close to heaven as anyone has ever gotten before actually going there, Israel was busy raising hell down below.

It wasn't as if Moses was gone for a year. But 40 days was all it took for spiritual amnesia to set in and for the people of

Israel to completely turn their backs on God by indulging in all kinds of debauchery. Not only did they forget God, but they also replaced him with a golden calf and even credited the statue for rescuing them from Egypt.

Another instance of Israel's struggle to trust God occurred when Moses sent 12 spies (one from each tribe) on a 40-day mission to explore the land of Canaan (aka the Promised Land). On day 41, 10 of the spies returned with a negative report because the giants they had seen seemed bigger than the miracles behind them. Their stubborn focus on the negative blinded them to the memory of God's overwhelming faithfulness. Joshua and Caleb were the only two spies who returned with a favorable report because they hadn't forgotten how big their God was. Their response to whether Israel could seize the land was the same as the catchphrase that comedic actor Rob Schneider made famous: "You can do it!"

Unfortunately, the negative report of the other 10 spies generated fear throughout Israel and incited a rebellion. This resulted in 40 years of wandering in the wilderness—one year for each day the spies had explored the land. This is the very reason that only a new generation of Israelites (with the exception of Joshua and Caleb) entered the Promised Land.

ELIJAH FORGOT

Elijah was one of God's greatest spokespersons, and he experienced numerous supernatural miracles because his faith was strong. He heard God, obeyed God, and was used mightily by God to demonstrate his marvelous wonders. Elijah announced that it wouldn't rain in his region for three years—and it didn't. Then there was the time when Elijah was fed by birds—apparently, they flew in takeout from somewhere. God also used Elijah to multiply a widow's flour and olive oil, and he later raised her son from the dead.

My favorite Elijah story is about the time he had a showdown with 850 false prophets on Mount Carmel to prove who the one true God was. Elijah and the prophets agreed that the winner would be whoever called down fire from the sky. Elijah let the other guys go first, so they prepared their altar and sacrifice and began calling on their false gods.

No response. Nothing.

When Elijah mocked them, suggesting that perhaps their god was taking a bathroom break, the prophets began cutting themselves while dancing around the altar chanting their incantations.[15] I can imagine they were ready to lose their minds until, bloodied and dejected, they finally conceded.

Next it was Elijah's turn. He raised the stakes by digging a trench around his altar. Then he cut up a bull, threw it on the altar, dumped water on it, and even filled up the trench.

Think about Elijah's resolve. His confidence in God was rock solid. He was the kind of dude I would have wanted to hang around with. He simply called upon God, and God came through—raining down fire from the sky that licked up the water and completely consumed the sacrifice. How's that for showing up and showing off?

Boom goes the dynamite . . . for real!

Then Elijah slaughtered all 850 false prophets! (#BringTheBoom)

Then the story takes an even more bizarre turn.

When wicked Queen Jezebel heard that Elijah had killed all her prophets, she threatened his life. Elijah's response to the queen's threat was absolutely mind-boggling when you consider the miracle of God that he had just witnessed firsthand.

Elijah ran. He didn't just run—he ran all day, scared for his life! Then he plopped down under a tree and asked God to take his life.

Say what?

Dude, you just killed hundreds of bad guys!

How did he forget so fast? How did he fall so far?

I can't be too quick to point the finger. I have done the exact same thing. I have experienced some unbelievable times when God has revealed himself powerfully during one of our church services, when people have given their lives to Christ and have gone home celebrating Jesus and talking about how awesome the service was and how amazing our church is . . . and then I have fallen into a full-blown depression on Monday morning when faced with conflict.

Have you done the same thing? Perhaps you're there right now. I want to tell you the same thing that God sent an angel to tell Elijah: "Get up!"

GET UP!

A few weeks ago, my family and I spent the evening playing the card game Uno. Instead of playing individually, we divided into two teams—our 11-year-old daughter, Savannah, and me versus Annette and our 8-year-old son, Ashton.

Savannah and I breezed through round one and won—but only because I cheated. No one knew I had cheated, including Savannah. Still, I celebrated and made a big deal of our victory! My son, who is still learning how to lose gracefully, wasn't very happy. I didn't care. I rubbed it in. (I know, I know. Dad of the Year, right?)

Don't worry. I confessed that I had cheated, and we all had a good laugh after I explained how I'd pulled it off.

Shuffle. Rematch.

Our second game lasted much longer. We made our way through the entire deck before Ashton and Annette eventually won fair and square. Immediately, my son began running around the room to take his Uno victory lap. His whooping and hollering looked more like an NFL end-zone celebration than anything.

C'mon, bro! Chill out!

Nope. Not a chance.

Apparently, he was just getting started. The more I tried to settle him down—*Dude! It's just a game!*—the more he escalated his victory celebration. But when he started bouncing up and down, shaking his booty at his sister and me, and screaming, "Oh yeah! Oh yeah!" I decided to give him a taste of his own medicine. Jumping up onto my chair, I began a little chicken dance of my own.

Well, my craziness went unintentionally to the next level when I lost my balance, the chair toppled over, and I landed on top of it with my ribs taking the brunt of the force. The impact knocked the air out me, and I ended up lying in a heap on the floor—practically in tears from the pain—while my family was practically in tears from laughing at me.

That's a funny story, but it's not funny to have life knock you down for real, or to have the enemy standing over you, gloating and mocking.

Ha, ha! Forty-one didn't come!
Ha, ha! God's not listening!
Ha, ha! You're finished!

"My enemies, don't be glad because of my troubles! I may have fallen, but I will get up; I may be sitting in the dark, but the LORD is my light." It ain't over. *Get up!*

When that happens, fight back with the words of the prophet Micah: "My enemies, don't be glad because of my troubles! I may have fallen, but I will get up; I may be sitting in the dark, but the LORD is my light."[16]

Remember, don't put a period where God put a comma.

It ain't over.

Get up!

#41WillCome

MY 50 FAVORITE 40s

If you conduct a topical search of the word *forty* in the New Living Translation of the Bible, you will find 92 results. This means there are 92 opportunities to find meaning in day 41 or year 41. Because *41 Will Come* unlocks the biblical significance of the number 41 and illustrates what it represents, here is a list of my 50 favorite references to the number 40 that will help you in your own studies. The following verses are all taken from the New Living Translation.

1. Genesis 7:4
Seven days from now I will make the rains pour down on the earth. And it will rain for forty days and forty nights, until I have wiped from the earth all the living things I have created.

2. Genesis 7:12
The rain continued to fall for forty days and forty nights.

3. Genesis 7:17
For forty days the floodwaters grew deeper, covering the ground and lifting the boat high above the earth.

4. Genesis 8:6
After another forty days, Noah opened the window he had made in the boat.

5. Exodus 16:35
So the people of Israel ate manna for forty years until they arrived at the land where they would settle. They ate manna until they came to the border of the land of Canaan.

6. Exodus 24:18
Moses disappeared into the cloud as he climbed higher up the mountain. He remained on the mountain forty days and forty nights.

7. Exodus 34:28
Moses remained there on the mountain with the LORD forty days and forty nights. In all that time he ate no bread and drank no water. And the LORD wrote the terms of the covenant—the Ten Commandments—on the stone tablets.

8. Numbers 13:25
After exploring the land for forty days, the men returned.

9. Numbers 14:33
Your children will be like shepherds, wandering in the wilderness for forty years. In this way, they will pay for your faithlessness, until the last of you lies dead in the wilderness.

10. Numbers 14:34

Because your men explored the land for forty days, you must wander in the wilderness for forty years—a year for each day, suffering the consequences of your sins. Then you will discover what it is like to have me for an enemy.

11. Numbers 32:13

The LORD was angry with Israel and made them wander in the wilderness for forty years until the entire generation that sinned in the Lord's sight had died.

12. Deuteronomy 1:3

Forty years after the Israelites left Egypt, on the first day of the eleventh month, Moses addressed the people of Israel, telling them everything the LORD had commanded him to say.

13. Deuteronomy 2:7

The LORD your God has blessed you in everything you have done. He has watched your every step through this great wilderness. During these forty years, the LORD your God has been with you, and you have lacked nothing.

14. Deuteronomy 8:2

Remember how the LORD your God led you through the wilderness for these forty years, humbling you and testing you to prove your character, and to find out whether or not you would obey his commands.

15. Deuteronomy 8:4

For all these forty years your clothes didn't wear out, and your feet didn't blister or swell.

16. Deuteronomy 9:9

This happened when I was on the mountain receiving the tablets of stone inscribed with the words of the covenant that the LORD had made with you. I was there for forty days and forty nights, and all that time I ate no food and drank no water.

17. Deuteronomy 9:11

At the end of the forty days and nights, the LORD handed me the two stone tablets inscribed with the words of the covenant.

18. Deuteronomy 9:18

Then, as before, I threw myself down before the LORD for forty days and nights. I ate no bread and drank no water because of the great sin you had committed by doing what the LORD hated, provoking him to anger.

19. Deuteronomy 9:25

That is why I threw myself down before the LORD for forty days and nights—for the LORD said he would destroy you.

20. Deuteronomy 10:10

As for me, I stayed on the mountain in the LORD's presence for forty days and nights, as I had done the first time. And once again the LORD listened to my pleas and agreed not to destroy you.

21. Deuteronomy 29:5
For forty years I led you through the wilderness, yet your clothes and sandals did not wear out.

22. Joshua 5:6
The Israelites had traveled in the wilderness for forty years until all the men who were old enough to fight in battle when they left Egypt had died. For they had disobeyed the LORD, and the LORD vowed he would not let them enter the land he had sworn to give us—a land flowing with milk and honey.

23. Joshua 14:7
I was forty years old when Moses, the servant of the LORD, sent me from Kadesh-barnea to explore the land of Canaan. I returned and gave an honest report.

24. Judges 3:11-12
So there was peace in the land for forty years. Then Othniel son of Kenaz died. Once again the Israelites did evil in the LORD's sight.

25. Judges 13:1
Again the Israelites did evil in the LORD's sight, so the Lord handed them over to the Philistines, who oppressed them for forty years.

26. 1 Samuel 4:18
When the messenger mentioned what had happened to the Ark of God, Eli fell backward from his seat beside the gate. He broke his neck and died, for he was old and overweight. He had been Israel's judge for forty years.

27. 1 Samuel 17:16
For forty days, every morning and evening, the Philistine champion strutted in front of the Israelite army.

28. 2 Samuel 5:4
David was thirty years old when he began to reign, and he reigned forty years in all.

29. 1 Kings 2:11
David had reigned over Israel for forty years, seven of them in Hebron and thirty-three in Jerusalem.

30. 1 Kings 11:42
Solomon ruled in Jerusalem over all Israel for forty years.

31. 1 Kings 19:8
So he got up and ate and drank, and the food gave him enough strength to travel forty days and forty nights to Mount Sinai, the mountain of God.

32. 2 Kings 12:1
Joash began to rule over Judah in the seventh year of King

Jehu's reign in Israel. He reigned in Jerusalem forty years. His mother was Zibiah from Beersheba.

33. 1 Chronicles 29:27

He reigned over Israel for forty years, seven of them in Hebron and thirty-three in Jerusalem.

34. 2 Chronicles 24:1

Joash was seven years old when he became king, and he reigned in Jerusalem forty years. His mother was Zibiah from Beersheba.

35. Nehemiah 9:21

For forty years you sustained them in the wilderness, and they lacked nothing. Their clothes did not wear out, and their feet did not swell!

36. Psalm 95:10

For forty years I was angry with them, and I said, "They are a people whose hearts turn away from me. They refuse to do what I tell them."

37. Ezekiel 29:11-13

For forty years not a soul will pass that way, neither people nor animals. It will be completely uninhabited. I will make Egypt desolate, and it will be surrounded by other desolate nations. Its cities will be empty and desolate for forty years, surrounded by other ruined cities. I will scatter the Egyptians to distant lands. But this is what the Sovereign

Lord also says: "At the end of the forty years I will bring the Egyptians home again from the nations to which they have been scattered."

38. Amos 2:10
It was I who rescued you from Egypt and led you through the desert for forty years, so you could possess the land of the Amorites.

39. Jonah 3:4
On the day Jonah entered the city, he shouted to the crowds: "Forty days from now Nineveh will be destroyed!"

40. Matthew 4:2
For forty days and forty nights he fasted and became very hungry.

41. Mark 1:13
He was tempted by Satan for forty days. He was out among the wild animals, and angels took care of him.

42. Luke 4:2
He was tempted by the devil for forty days. Jesus ate nothing all that time and became very hungry.

43. Acts 1:3
During the forty days after he suffered and died, he appeared to the apostles from time to time, and he proved to them in

many ways that he was actually alive. And he talked to them about the Kingdom of God.

44. Acts 7:30
Forty years later, in the desert near Mount Sinai, an angel appeared to Moses in the flame of a burning bush.

45. Acts 7:36
And by means of many wonders and miraculous signs, he led them out of Egypt, through the Red Sea, and through the wilderness for forty years.

46. Acts 7:42
Then God turned away from them and abandoned them to serve the stars of heaven as their gods! In the book of the prophets it is written, "Was it to me you were bringing sacrifices and offerings during those forty years in the wilderness, Israel?"

47. Acts 13:18
He put up with them through forty years of wandering in the wilderness.

48. Acts 13:21
The people begged for a king, and God gave them Saul son of Kish, a man of the tribe of Benjamin, who reigned for forty years.

49. Hebrews 3:9
There your ancestors tested and tried my patience, even though they saw my miracles for forty years.

50. Hebrews 3:17
Who made God angry for forty years? Wasn't it the people who sinned, whose corpses lay in the wilderness?

Notes

CHAPTER 1: PATS AND POSTPONED DREAMS
1. Daniel 11:32, ESV.
2. Luke 5:12, NIV.

CHAPTER 2: FEE FI FO FUM
1. 1 Samuel 16:12, NLT.
2. 1 Samuel 16:13, NLT.
3. Isaiah 43:1-3, NLT.
4. Perry Noble, "About NewSpring," PerryNoble.com (blog), https://perrynoble.com/about.
5. Acts 10:34, NLT.

CHAPTER 3: TOUGHER THAN HELL
1. 1 Samuel 17:36, NIV.
2. Matthew 19:26, CEV.
3. 1 John 4:4, CEV.
4. See Jeremiah 29:11.
5. Ephesians 2:10, NLT.
6. Romans 8:9-11, NLT.
7. Romans 8:31-39, MSG. Italics in original.
8. John 12:31, NIV.
9. 1 John 4:4, NLT.
10. NLT.
11. Matthew 16:18, NLT.

CHAPTER 4: CAN YOU HEAR ME NOW?

1. 1 Samuel 17:20-25, NLT.
2. 1 Samuel 17:16, NLT. Italics added.
3. 1 Samuel 17:25, NLT.
4. Ephesians 6:12, NLT.
5. 1 Peter 5:8, NLT.
6. Luke 22:31, MSG.
7. 1 Peter 5:8-9, MSG.
8. Ephesians 6:18, MSG.
9. Romans 8:1-2, NLT.
10. Ephesians 6:11, NLT. Italics added.
11. Ephesians 6:10, NIV.
12. 1 Peter 5:8-9, NLT.
13. See Matthew 16:23 and Mark 8:33.
14. Mark 16:7, NLT. Italics added.
15. See Acts 1:1-9.
16. See Acts 2.
17. Revelation 3:1-3, NIV.
18. 1 Peter 5:9, MSG.
19. Psalm 46:10, NLT.
20. Psalm 46:2-3, 6, NLT.
21. Bill Ward, "In One of the World's Quietest Rooms," Minneapolis *Star Tribune*, April 25, 2012, www.startribune.com/in-one-of-the-world-s-quietest-rooms/148924995.
22. Ibid.
23. Rachel Swatman, "Microsoft Lab Sets New Record for World's Quietest Place," *Officially Amazing* (blog), *Guinness World Records*, October 2, 2015, www.guinnessworldrecords.com/news/2015/10/microsoft-lab-sets-new-record-for-the-worlds-quietest-place-399444.
24. See Romans 10:17.
25. 2 Timothy 2:15, NKJV.
26. 1 Peter 5:9, MSG.
27. See Hebrews 10:25.
28. Hebrews 10:25, CEV.
29. Jude 1:20, NLT.

CHAPTER 5: TEN-FOUR, GOOD BUDDY!

1. 1 Samuel 17:28, NLT.
2. 1 Samuel 17:29, NKJV.
3. Psalm 37:4, ESV.
4. Ephesians 2:10, ESV.
5. Proverbs 29:18, MSG.

6. Matthew 20:26, CEV.
7. Nehemiah 1:1-11, NLT.
8. Nehemiah 8:10, NLT.
9. Psalm 17:4-5, MSG. Italics in original.
10. See Exodus 17:8-13.
11. Habakkuk 2:2-3, NLT.
12. "Study Focuses on Strategies for Achieving Goals, Resolutions," Dominican University of California News Room; http://www.dominican.edu/dominicannews/study-highlights-strategies-for-achieving-goals.
13. "Emmitt Smith Hall of Fame speech," ESPN.com, August 7, 2010, http://espn.go.com/blog/nfceast/print?id=16456&imagesPrint=off.
14. John C. Maxwell, *The 21 Most Powerful Minutes in a Leader's Day* (Nashville: Thomas Nelson, 2000), 226.

CHAPTER 6: SMASHMOUTH
1. NLT.
2. Mark Twain, *Pudd'nhead Wilson* (Mineola, NY: Dover Publications, 1999), 60.
3. Psalm 91:2, 4, 11, NLT.
4. Exodus 4:1-17, NLT.
5. Psalm 147:6, MSG.
6. Micah 7:8, NLT.
7. Psalm 34:4, NLT.
8. "Rev. Samuel Rodriguez," the National Hispanic Christian Leadership Conference, https://nhclc.org/about-us/rev-samuel-rodriguez.
9. Psalm 125:1, NLT.
10. Zechariah 4:10, NLT.
11. 2 Timothy 1:7, NLT.

CHAPTER 7: SHAKE IT OFF!
1. 1 Samuel 17:33, CEV.
2. 1 Corinthians 15:33, NLT.
3. 1 Corinthians 15:33, CEV.
4. Joel Osteen, *Become a Better You: Seven Keys to Improving Your Life Every Day* (New York: Free Press, 2007), 16.
5. Acts 5:29, NLT.
6. Mark 10:47, ESV.
7. Proverbs 13:12, NLT.
8. Mark 10:49, NLT.
9. Mark 10:51, NLT.
10. Philippians 4:8, NLT.
11. See Jeremiah 29:11 and Ephesians 2:10.

263

12. Psalm 139:14, ESV.
13. Psalm 5:12, NLT.
14. Psalm 147:6, MSG.
15. Psalm 1:6, MSG.
16. Psalm 147:4-5, MSG.
17. Psalm 46:1, NLT.
18. Matthew 12:34, ESV.
19. 1 John 5:4, ESV.
20. Judges 6:12, author's paraphrase.
21. Judges 6:15, author's paraphrase.
22. Judges 6:16, CEV.
23. 2 Corinthians 11:23-27, MSG.
24. See Acts 28:3.
25. 2 Corinthians 11:28, author's paraphrase.
26. 2 Corinthians 11:28-29, MSG.
27. Philippians 4:4, ESV.

CHAPTER 8: RAWK STANCE
1. "Iverson Practice!" YouTube video, 2:22, from an interview broadcast by CNN on May 7, 2002, posted by gordievsky, April 15, 2006, https://www.youtube.com/watch?v=eGDBR2L5kzI.
2. 1 Samuel 17:34-36, NLT.
3. John C. Maxwell, *The 21 Most Powerful Minutes in a Leader's Day* (Nashville: Thomas Nelson, 2000), 10.
4. 1 Corinthians 9:25, NLT.
5. Hebrews 12:11, NLT.
6. This is a popular rendition of a saying attributed to Lao-tzu (604 BC–531 BC).
7. See Exodus 8:9-10.
8. "Famous Quotations from Thomas Edison," the Edison Innovation Foundation, www.thomasedison.org/index.php/education/edison-quotes.
9. Ivan Maisel, "Spartans Kick Bruins to the Curb," ESPN, http://m.espn.go.com/ncf/grid/drawer?ceId=10151983&wjb.
10. Ephesians 6:11-13, NIV. Italics added.
11. 1 Peter 5:8, NIV.
12. Ephesians 6:13-18, NLT.
13. Genesis 39:9, NLT.
14. Genesis 50:20, NLT.

CHAPTER 9: *BOOM* GOES THE DYNAMITE!
1. Matthew 4:3-11, MSG.
2. Daniel 9:23, author's paraphrase.
3. Jeremiah 23:29, NLT.

4. Matthew 8:7-10, NLT. Italics added.
5. Psalm 23:4, ESV. Italics added.
6. 1 Samuel 17:43, NLT.
7. 1 Samuel 17:44, NLT.
8. 1 Samuel 17:45, NLT.
9. Ibid.
10. 1 Samuel 17:46, NLT.
11. Job 22:26-28, NASB.
12. Job 22:21-23, 26-28, NLT.
13. Joel Osteen, *I Declare: 31 Promises to Speak over Your Life* (New York: FaithWords, 2012), Day 17.
14. Daniel 11:32, NKJV.
15. Daniel 11:32, ESV.
16. Mayo Clinic Staff, "Brachial Plexus Injury: Overview," and "Brachial Plexus Injury: Symptoms and Causes," the Mayo Clinic online, www.mayoclinic.org/diseases-conditions/brachial-plexus-injury/home/ovc-20127336 and www.mayoclinic.org/diseases-conditions/brachial-plexus-injury/symptoms-causes/dxc-20127374.
17. Proverbs 18:21, ESV.
18. Proverbs 13:12, NIV.
19. Ibid. Italics added.
20. Mark 11:13-14, NLT.
21. Mark 11:20-25, NLT.
22. Mark 11:24, NLT.
23. Mark 4:35-40, NLT.

CHAPTER 10: RECKLESS CHARGE
1. Psalm 18:29, NLT.
2. Joshua 3:1-4, NLT.
3. Joshua 3:5, NLT.
4. Joshua 3:7-8, NLT.
5. Joshua 3:9-11, NLT.
6. Joshua 3:12-13, NLT.
7. See James 2:26.
8. Joshua 3:14-17, NLT.
9. Kathryn Schulz, "The Really Big One," *The New Yorker*, July 20, 2015, www.newyorker.com/magazine/2015/07/20/the-really-big-one.
10. Matthew 14:27, NLT.
11. Matthew 14:28, NLT.
12. Matthew 14:29, author's paraphrase.
13. Psalm 34:1, NLT.
14. Psalm 34:1-8, NLT. Italics added.

CHAPTER 11: WE WIN!

1. Proverbs 10:24-25, NLT.
2. Proverbs 24:10, NKJV.
3. Philippians 4:4, NIV.
4. Proverbs 16:3, NLT.
5. Dave Eminian, "Cowdrey Walks Plank," *Peoria Journal Star*, May 13, 2009, www.pjstar.com/article/20090513/NEWS/305139836.

CHAPTER 12: WHEN 41 DOESN'T COME

1. Dolly Gleason, "Tears That You Don't See," copyright © 2014 by Dolly Gleason. All rights reserved. Used by permission.
2. For more information about the World Race, see www.worldrace.org.
3. Psalm 34:18, NLT.
4. Isaiah 43:1-3, MSG.
5. Exodus 17:12-14, NLT.
6. 1 Corinthians 12:26, NIV.
7. CEV.
8. Jessilyn Justice, "Dwayne 'The Rock' Johnson: Faith Helped Me Battle Depression," *CharismaNews*, December 3, 2015, www.charismanews .com/culture/53604-dwayne-the-rock-johnson-faith-helped-me-battle -depression.
9. Ephesians 2:10, ESV.
10. Jeremiah 33:3, NIV.
11. Habakkuk 2:3, NLT.
12. Johann Wolfgang von Goethe, quoted in Thomas Carlyle, "Modern Culture," in *The Quarterly Review*, vol. 137, July & October 1874 (London: John Murray, 1874), 392.
13. Isaiah 43:16-17, MSG.
14. Zechariah 4:10, NLT.
15. See 1 Kings 18:27-28.
16. Micah 7:8, CEV.

Acknowledgments

I've dreamed about writing these acknowledgments for a long time, so I'm pretty sure I can write a chapter on gratitude and fill the pages with the countless names of those who have helped me along the way on this publishing journey. In fact, I want to encourage *you* to take some time to acknowledge those in your own life right now who have come alongside you to encourage you and hold up your arms. (#HelpPeopleWin)

HERE'S MY LIST:

Annette: We will celebrate 20 years of marriage right after this book releases. I am looking forward to celebrating our 41st in the distant future. Thank you for holding up my arms, laughing at my jokes, and letting me wear a man-bun around the house. (#ForeverYours)

Savannah and Ashton: My heart swells with pride just thinking about you and how much you have changed my life. It also makes my heart happy that you love Jesus and you enjoy serving his church. You make me grin from ear to ear when you point out the number 41 any time and every time you randomly see it. (#DaddyLovesYou)

Dad and Mom: I'm so grateful that you raised me not only to love Jesus but also to believe his Word. You have demonstrated what it means to stand by faith and boldly declare, "41 will come!" (#You'reTheBest)

Cherie and Eddy (and Jadea and Briella): Thank you for allowing me to share your story and for letting me be a part of it. Cherie, you will always be my 10-year-old birthday gift. Eddy, I'm immensely blessed to have you in our family. (#GoLiverpool)

Denny: I'm so glad that you're my brother. Our inside jokes will never end. (#TrudyForPresident)

Diana: I am thankful to have you as my mother-in-law, and I'm grateful for your constant encouragement. Thank you for making me smile by sending me daily inspiration via Pinterest and YouTube. (#NoMoreCatVideos)

Tate Clan: Uncle Bill and Aunt Marna (and Kendra and Steph), Uncle Hank and Aunt Val (and Jason and Heather), Uncle Mike and Aunt Pam (and Mike and Sue), I love you all. Thank you, Kendra, for the writing inspiration via beach photos. (#BringOnAirHockey)

David Chatburn: Thank you for being my mom's cousin . . . and mine. (#WinkWink)

RockChurch: I can't thank you enough for your genuine support and constant encouragement. I wouldn't want to be anywhere else. (#TheBestIsYetToCome)

RC Staff and Board of Directors: Catherine Worden, Chad and Tara Ingham, Chris and Melody Papazis, Cory and Sarah Vance, Lance and Jeri Van Tine, Theresa and Michael Noel, Jason and Sarah Williams, Mike and Nancy Winstead, Mike and Leann Crall, I cannot believe we get to do this together! Thank you for your leadership, wisdom, counsel, service, and faithfulness. I absolutely love doing life and ministry alongside all of you! (#DreamTeam)

Jim Powell: Little did I know that your invite to the 2013 Re:Write Conference would result in this. I am grateful for your leadership, mentorship, friendship . . . and all the other ships. Thank you, thank you, thank you! (#DirtMatters)

Ted Dekker: Thank you for building a platform (Re:Write Conference) that turns hopes deferred into dreams fulfilled. (#Proverbs13:12)

The Fedd Agency: Esther, first of all, thank you for launching the Re:Write Conference! In 2013 I asked you for 60 seconds to share my concept. You gave me more. Your favorable feedback fueled my confidence to submit a proposal. It's an absolute honor to be represented by you. You are truly a rock star. Whitney, you have been a tremendous lifeline for me behind the scenes. Thank you for your wisdom, input, direction, encouragement, and for replying graciously to my endless e-mails and questions. (#FeddUpwardAndOnward)

Tyndale Momentum: Jan, I will never forget the moment when you announced my name at Re:Write. Ever. Thank you for believing in #41WillCome and organizing the best publishing team ever. I am honored and thrilled to partner with Tyndale. Sharon, you are a breath of fresh air and have helped me feel at ease during this process. Sarah and Jillian, thank you for your wisdom, input, and encouragement—and for holding the hand of a first-time author during this journey. Nancy, Cassidy, and Maggie, you ladies are awesome. Maggie, your enthusiasm is contagious! Dean, you hit the cover design out of the ballpark! Dave, thank you for your priceless wisdom, for your editorial input and edits, for teaching me to embrace the color red, and for tolerating my obsession with hashtags. I thoroughly enjoyed the editing process with you—especially your comments and interjections. (#TeamTyndaleRocks)

Chad Allen: Not only was Book Proposal Academy a timely divine appointment, but your expertise, input, genuine feedback, and personal touch proved instrumental in helping me craft my official book proposal. (#BPALifer)

Mark Batterson: Your inspirational talk at the Re:Write Conference in 2013 pushed me to move from dreaming to doing. When you mentioned my book during your talk at Re:Write 2015, it moved me to tears. Thank you! (#PrayingCirclesAround41)

Kurt Bubna and Cherie Lowe: Thank you for your willingness to walk this rookie through the ballpark. (#ReWriteCommonDenominator)

Eastman Curtis: Thank you for believing in me, trusting me with opportunities, and teaching me to dream big! (#KickingDevilHeinie)

Angel Curtis: Thank you for believing in me and pushing me to be better. Your amazing generosity and overall wisdom have influenced me more than I can ever say. (#WisdomWoman)

My sincere gratitude for allowing me to share part of your story: Tim and Maureen Gray; Amanda Patterson; Eddy and Cherie Eddyto; Arlie, Judy, and Anthony Neaville; Dan and Cherity Helfers; Jill Lulay; Dane Lulay; John and Julie McVey; Linda Hunt; Cory and Sarah Vance; and Dolly Gleason. (#YourStoryMatters)

Virtual high fives and fist bumps: Debbie Seaborn, Jim Kochenberger, Bob and Debbie Starr, Charles and Marissa Golden, Cecil Dickson, Mike Lindsey, Dave Mudd, Sean Keith, Joe Paris, Roger Schenck, Todd Swardenski, Bruce Cowdrey, Bob Beeman, Bill Scheer, Don Grosvenor, Blaine Bartel, Bill Allison, Tom Elmore, Jamie Markley, John King,

Brian Sanders, Bob Martin, Mike Womer, Benny Perez, Scott Mendenhall, Amanda Noelle Wilcox, John Bishop, Kurt Wiegand, Jim and Beckie Poole, Juan Rios, Mike Gallas, Seth Lowe, Julie Lyles Carr, Jay Ingham, Billy "Walk-around-the-Block" Kocher, Pete and Kim Hutchinson, Jim Les, Matthew Barnett, Pizza Ranch, Peoria Christian School, Scott Seynemeier and the Ski and Grow gang, my Focus Group family, and my official #41WillCome Prayer Team. (#WootWootWoot)

About the Author

CHUCK TATE is the founder and lead pastor of RockChurch, a growing and thriving congregation in the heart of Illinois. Before planting RockChurch in 1998, Chuck worked for a national youth ministry in Tulsa, Oklahoma. In that role, he managed and spoke at conventions across the United States and Canada and coproduced a national television program that aired on Trinity Broadcasting Network. Chuck and his wife, Annette, are the parents of Savannah and Ashton.